gen X 1965 - 1981
gen Y 1982 - 1995
gen Z 1996 -

what is our culture.
relationships
need a web page
e books link
photo's & personal/comments
stories
give peps something to talk about

Knowing

Engage
the Next
Generation
Now

SARAH L. SLADEK

association
management
press

WASHINGTON, DC

The author has worked diligently to ensure that all information in this book is accurate as of the time of publication and consistent with standards of good practice in the general management community. As research and practice advance, however, standards may change. For this reason it is recommended that readers evaluate the applicability of any recommendations in light of particular situations and changing standards.

ASAE: The Center for Association Leadership
1575 I Street, NW
Washington, DC 20005-1103
Phone: (202) 626-2723; (888) 950-2723 outside metropolitan Washington, DC area
Fax: (202) 220-6439
Email: books@asaecenter.org

We connect great ideas and great people to inspire leadership and achievement in the association community.

Keith C. Skillman, CAE, Vice President, Publications, ASAE: The Center for Association Leadership
Baron Williams, CAE, Director of Book Publishing, ASAE: The Center for Association Leadership

Cover by Beth Lower, Art Director, ASAE: The Center for Association Leadership
Interior design by Troy Scott Parker, Cimarron Design

This book is available at a special discount when ordered in bulk quantities. For information, contact the ASAE Member Service Center at (202) 371-0940. A complete catalog of titles is available on the ASAE website at www.asaecenter.org.

ISBN-13: 978-0-88034-372-5

Printed in the United States of America.

10 9 8 7 6 5 4 3 2 1

The book is dedicated to the first generation of the
Post-Industrial Era—may you have the courage and wisdom
to preserve the best of our traditions, to innovate and launch
new strategies and enterprises, to hold the older generations
to a higher standard, and to create a better future for us all.

◆

Thank you Kris, Cathy, and Shawna for leading adventurous,
meaningful lives and inspiring me to do the same.

And once again I thank my husband and our bright and
beautiful daughters for their unwavering faith, love,
and constant laughter. You brighten my every day.

CONTENTS

INTRODUCTION

This book isn't just about a generation. It's about change; the kind of change that only comes around every hundred years or so.

Generation Y (individuals born within the years of 1982 and 1995) has come of age during a time of economic recession, digital innovation, and political revolution. All too often we refer to this change as being purely driven by technology, but that's not the case at all. In fact, this book illuminates five currents of change that are so powerful that they have been referred to as economies. The Sharing Economy, Gig Economy, Knowledge Economy, Experience Economy, and Impact Economy are spurring unprecedented social, economic, and political change on a global scale.

Not surprising, these economies have shaped the opinions, values, and behaviors of Generation Y in radical ways—which will undoubtedly shape *every* generation's opinions, values, and behaviors and have already begun to do so. It's the Trickle-Up Effect. Sooner or later, the youngest generation influences the older generations, and this is how widespread change often occurs.

Right now, everything about the way we live, work, and do business is changing. What really bothers me (terrifies me, actually) is not the change itself; it's the fact that almost all of our nation's established organizations are struggling with the concept of change or are flat-out reluctant to change.

Take a look around. With the exception of the technology industry, nearly all the power is held by one generation in every sector in every corner of the world. Our political, business, government, nonprofit, and education leaders are graying and the systems and processes themselves often are outdated. Peter Cappelli, Professor of Management at the University of Pennsylvania's Wharton School and research associate at the National Bureau of Economic Research, has authored several articles in *Harvard Business Review* referring to the large, older, complex, and bureaucratic models from the 1950s still being utilized in business today, which have created an ongoing source of pain and have proven dysfunctional. "Every talent management process in use today was developed half a century ago," he wrote.

We're on the brink of the largest shift in human capital in history and no one seems to be paying any attention. The 2013 Nonprofit Employee Trends Survey and executive research conducted by Korn/Ferry and Deloitte all indicate that succession planning isn't a priority for 70 percent of the organizations out there. Generation Y is still being dismissed as too young and too entitled to assume any real responsibility.

Change is evolving all around us, yet in many ways organizations are still acting like it's 1989. This is risky business. If we fail to engage the future, we prepare to fail. It's that simple.

Maybe I wrote this book because I empathize with Generation Y.

As a Gen Xer, my generation didn't have a smooth transition into adulthood. We were dismissed as "slackers" as we struggled to get jobs during an era when layoffs and mergers were running rampant. We've never known job security and we've lived through four recessions, struggling to pay off college debts while also paying for ridiculously high-priced childcare and mortgages. As the sandwich generation, many Gen Xers are caring for aging relatives while caring for children under the age of 18. Psychologists say we're the most stressed-out generation and economists say we'll never be able to afford the quality of life our parents afforded.

My generation was kicked when we were down. We're renowned for being more cynical, defensive, and sarcastic as a result, and maybe that's true. But we did stand up to our demanding bosses who expected us to work overtime and we successfully introduced the idea of work–life balance. As we move into management, most of my peers are hopeful they will lead with more compassion than our predecessors, recalling how difficult it was for us to establish ourselves.

So I understand what it's like to be a Gen Y, dismissed as "entitled" or labeled the "failure to launch" generation when the chips are stacked against you.

I also wrote this book because, quite frankly, I don't like the direction that organizations are headed and I fear there are going to be considerable ramifications. In the United States, not unlike many countries worldwide, we are holding steadfast to traditions, the concept of hierarchy, and the idea that wisdom and talent is accompanied solely by experience. That may have been true in the past, but that's simply not the case anymore. Inclusion is our best and only option and I fear we'll hit rock bottom and have a revolution on our hands before we embrace the participation of the younger generation and warm up to the idea of change.

I've had the opportunity to work with hundreds of membership associations worldwide, and there's no denying associations are challenged to change, which is why they are challenged to reach Generation Y. The same challenge has emerged in workplaces and governments worldwide.

However, the more you learn about Generation Y, the more you realize this generation is an accurate representation of the complex and significant changes of their youth. This generation is a product of their environment and they have been shaped with entirely new skillsets, opinions, and values. They won't go back to base on anything because they don't know the Old World of the Industrial Age; they are settlers of the New World shaped by five emerging, prominent, and intersecting economies. It may seem like they are always steering us away from traditions, when in fact they are steering us towards what's relevant and meaningful in this brand new world.

This isn't just about a young demographic coming into power and the need to understand "how to deal with kids these days." The more you learn about Generation Y, the more you can comprehend and appreciate the significance of the economic, political, and social change happening all around us. The more you learn about Generation Y, the easier it is to determine the best path for going forward.

To be honest, I have studied generations for 12 years, and even I didn't expect to discover that Generation Y's arrival was so closely aligned with so many powerful economic transitions. I seriously doubt the arrival of a single generation has ever ushered in this much transition at any other time in history. There is much to learn from this generation and much potential that has yet to be tapped.

I urge you, dear reader, to open your minds to the opportunities this "New World" generation provides. You just might be surprised to discover that knowing Generation Y is the same as knowing your own fate.

CHAPTER 1

Member Shift

"The importance of change is being seen.
Whether this will come soon enough and in
a sufficient degree is the big question."

Bas Huussen
Project Leader, Huussen Elektro
Board Member, Young Uneto-VNI (Holland)
Age: 32

In 2008, I was scheduled to speak on the topic of generations at a conference in Atlanta, but I never actually spoke.

The conference was hosted by a membership association with an incredible history dating back to its founding in 1919. Shortly prior to my presentation, I walked down to the ballroom. The doors were closed. I could hear a tremendous amount of noise coming from inside. While I was standing there, debating whether or not to walk in, someone from the registration desk ran over and asked me to wait in the hall.

So I waited and wondered what was going on. About five minutes before I was slated to speak, the event organizer emerged from the ballroom. She was frantic. Breathless and distracted, she told me the association leaders, including representatives from throughout the nation, were engaged in a private meeting that had run long and asked me to continue waiting.

Fifteen minutes later, the event organizer emerged again. This time around she invited me to join her. We walked into the ballroom, sat in the back, and I took in the site. The ballroom was full of 200 people, standing in clumps, talking loudly to one another. On the risers at the front, a small gathering of people sat at a table and podium. The song, *You Can't Stop the Beat*, from the 2007 film soundtrack of *Hairspray* was blaring over the sound system. Several members of the audience were singing along:

You can't stop today
As it comes speeding down the track
Child, yesterday is hist'ry

And it's never coming back …

'Cause you can't stop
The motion of the ocean
Or the sun in the sky
You can wonder if you wanna
But I never ask why
And if you try to hold me down
I'm gonna spit in your eye and say
That you can't stop the beat!

When the song ended, the debate ensued. The people in the audience were the firing squad. They were chapter leaders and members, taking aim at the board leaders sitting on the risers and occasionally at one another, too. Emotions were running high as the microphone was passed around and people expressed their heartfelt concerns, frustration, and anger.

The event organizer leaned over to me and said, "This has been going on for *hours*." She went on to explain the association was at risk of closing its doors because the association had lost considerable dues revenue. "Not enough young people joining," she summarized.

I reminded her that that was why I was there. "I can help," I told her eagerly. "My entire presentation addresses these issues everyone is talking about." She suggested we speak to the association CEO.

We made our way through the angry crowd and found the CEO, who was sitting quietly in the audience, observing what was unfolding before her and taking it all in. "I'm sorry we wasted your time," she said. "I don't know what's going to happen after today, but I think it's too late. I don't think we can be saved." And then she asked me to leave.

Ironic, isn't it? I was hired to speak to an association struggling to engage younger members, about how to engage younger members, and even in its time of greatest despair the association's leadership would only listen to its current members—the very ones struggling to solve the problem. They wasted time creating chaos, placing blame, feeling sorry for themselves, and putting a soundtrack to it.

Not long after that, I received notice that the association had closed its doors.

I can't help but think that was a miserable way to go. The last conference the association hosted, in its 89th year of existence, will forever go down in history as one of pandemonium, bitterness, and defeat.

Worse yet, the association's leadership gave up. Rather than revel in the pursuit of relevance and innovation and guide the association to higher ground, they let a civil war take place and threw in the towel. Evidently, they really believed change isn't possible; that truly, you can't stop the beat.

I disagree.

This book is going to outline numerous examples of associations, businesses, and other organizations who have managed to turn the tide in their favor simply by focusing on and creating relevance for one *1982-95* demographic. From an economic perspective, as well as a consumer, marketing, and management perspective there are strong cases that clearly demonstrate that this approach works.

I fully expect there will be people who will be somewhat alarmed by this idea and may even go so far as to dismiss it as stereotyping or segmentation, ignoring the substantial data and case studies to indicate otherwise. These leaders will choose to go back to burying their heads in the database, debating dues increases, and puzzling over the changing definition of engagement, all the while sinking further into quicksand.

That's unfortunate, because there isn't an organization out there that ever experienced long-term success by practicing the art of navel-gazing or close-mindedness. Truly I tell you, the opposite of evolution is extinction, and never before has that fact been more apparent.

Take a look around you and appreciate what's happening. We're living through an era of more change than at any other time in history, which is pretty fascinating in and of itself. And let's face it, being 20 years old today is way different than it was just 10 years ago. Time has changed everything—including our values.

Profiling Members Using Demographics

In her book, *The Art of Membership*, author Sheri Jacobs recommends profiling members according to what they value, rather than by demographic characteristics. I would make the case that one huge element of demographics—your generation—heavily influences your values; that associations aren't inclusive of the values of younger generations, and that's why membership is declining.

Interesting enough, as early as the 19th century philosophers studied generations and discovered the rapidity of social change in youth formed cohesive and distinct characteristics among groups of people born during a common period or era.

It was also discovered early on that as people age, their instinct of social conservation becomes stronger, which inevitably brings them into conflict with the normal attribute of youth, which is innovation.

In other words, it's natural for older generations to resist change, but this resistance can have negative side effects, not excluding generational differences and even conflict when interacting with younger generations who have an insatiable desire for innovation.

We're seeing that desire for social conservation come into play more than ever, likely because membership associations have pretty much followed the same recipe (charge dues, elect officers, hold meetings, repeat) since the first associations were founded in the 1600s. (It worked for this long—why wouldn't it work now? Associations have survived wars, plagues, and recessions for crying out loud! Certainly they can withstand the evolution of Facebook, right?)

The idea of change isn't an easy one to digest, but I think you already knew that.

For the past two centuries, philosophers, sociologists, and marketers, have studied generations and have come to the same conclusion: Generational values are largely shared by the people born during the same era and shaped by the social influences which take place during childhood and adolescence. Also, once those values are shaped, we tend to carry them throughout our lives and become rooted in, well, conserving them.

The study of generations presents powerful clues on where to start to faster connect with and influence people of different ages. Obviously, there are many factors that go into shaping an individual's experience, which is why everyone is unique. However, on the whole, those within a generation often exhibit surprisingly similar characteristics—and one of those characteristics shared by younger generations is the decline in membership involvement.

Membership decline isn't happening across the board with every generation. We're not reading headlines about Baby Boomers suddenly up and leaving their beloved associations. Rather, we're seeing countless reports of associations struggling to engage younger members.

For example, *USA Today* and *The New York Times* have been keeping tabs on the steep membership declines in service clubs and unions for the past several years. In 2012, the U.S. Chamber of Commerce Foundation published *The Millennial Generation Research Review,* which revealed 62% of professional associations were experiencing flat or declining membership, and associations with 5,000 or more members reported their greatest challenge is engaging the membership of younger generations. In 2014, Pew Research's *Millennials in Adulthood* study noted this generation has fewer attachments to traditional institutions.

This isn't merely a fluke or something that will suddenly correct itself. There's a reason why this is happening, and it's because the needs, interests, expectations—and values—of younger generations are considerably different than the generations that have come before them.

How to Engage Younger Generations

The challenge of engaging younger generations really started garnering attention in the 2000s. As Generation X came of age (1965–1981), it became increasingly obvious that engagement was changing and a member shift was underway.

- In 2000, Robert Putnam's book, *Bowling Alone: The Collapse and Revival of American Community,* cited data showing an aggregate decline in membership of traditional civic organizations, supporting his thesis that U.S. social capital had also declined.

- In 2004, declining membership became an urgent and highly publicized concern for all types of membership organizations. Media all over the world were covering stories about declining membership in everything from trade unions to scouting, churches, and veterans' organizations.

- In 2005, the *Journal of Association Leadership* explored the disappearance of the traditional association member base, classified as a white 50 to 60 year-old homeowner, with a higher education, urban-based, married, and with a higher-level job. The article urged associations to prepare for rapidly approaching, significant demographic shifts.

- In 2006, *The Washington Post* reported on declining membership engagement among Generation X. The article cited research funded by SmithBucklin and done by Arthur C. Brooks for The William E. Smith Institute for Association Research that projected Gen Xers would likely be interested in joining associations when they hit their peak earning years, but cautioned their participation was definitely "not a sure thing" because they wanted tangible services and real evidence that joining something is good for their careers.

- In 2010, National Public Radio reported on the robust history of trade associations in America, citing the fact that during the past 10 years many had struggled to survive.

- In 2011 at the annual meeting of the American Sociological Association, information was shared from a research project examining the overall decline in active memberships in civic groups, fraternal organizations, and other local associations since 1994. Research revealed that active membership had declined 6 percent; "generational differences" was cited as one of the reasons.

- 92 percent believe that business success should be measured by more than profit
  - Deloitte
- 81 percent have donated money, goods, or services
  - Walden University and Harris Interactive
- 80 percent prefer on-the-spot recognition over formal reviews
  - Achievers and Experience Inc.
- 75 percent of the global workforce by 2025
  - U.S. Bureau of Labor Statistics
- 70 percent have "friended" their managers and/or co-workers on Facebook
  - Cisco
- 63 percent have a bachelor's degree
  - Millennial Branding/PayScale
- 61 percent feel personally responsible to make a difference in the world
  - Huffington Post
- 56 percent wouldn't work for a company that bans social media
  - Cisco
- 50 percent want to start their own business or have already done so
  - Kauffman Foundation
- $45,000 is the average amount they carry in debt
  - PNC Financial Services
- 45 percent agree with preferential treatment to improve position of minorities
  - U.S. Chamber
- 43 percent have liked more than 20 brands on Facebook
  - Mr. Youth
- 40 percent of electorate by 2020
  - The Center for American Progress
- 39 percent have a tattoo
  - Pew Research
- $2.45 trillion expected to be their annual spending by 2018
  - Oracle
- 2 years is average employment tenure
  - Millennial Branding/PayScale

Here we are, 14 years after declining membership among younger generations emerged as newsworthy, and few associations are making headlines as hotbeds for radical change and skyrocketing engagement among younger generations.

What's shocking to me is that despite all the decline and decreases in engagement among younger generations, many association leaders remain adamant that this is just a phase and all this generational talk is just a lot of hot air with no real ramifications.

This denial has led to complacency and apathy and these associations have found themselves stuck in a rut of delivering the same old program, focusing on the same old issues, generating the same old knowledge, planning the same old conference, and managing the association in the same old way.

Meanwhile, the leadership bemoans the fact that membership is declining; that "kids today" possess little time or inclination to join them; and that the world is surely going to hell in a hand-basket.

That's the other part of the equation that is really shocking to me—the response to change, or lack thereof. I think it's safe to say the majority of the membership associations out there (excluding student associations) are run by Baby Boomers (1946–1964), a generation that influenced significant and rapid waves of change themselves.

As teens and young adults, the Boomers were criticized by their elders for being a generation consumed by sex, drugs, and rock 'n roll. In 1967, *Time* magazine ran an article about the Boomer generation, referring to them as "hippies" and stating: "to their deeply worried parents throughout the country, they seem more like dangerously deluded dropouts, candidates for a very sound spanking and a cram course in civics." Ouch.

Yes, this generation grew their hair and sported miniskirts. They were misunderstood and tagged as being incapable of doing much of anything, but this wave of 78 million people stood up for their beliefs, rallied for civil rights and women's rights, protested against President Nixon and the Vietnam War, and moved into positions of great influence and power.

Because they created and experienced change—and stereotypes—as young adults themselves, I would expect the Boomers to welcome the concept of change, and openly welcome the ideals and participation of younger generations, but that certainly hasn't been the norm. The Boomers seem to have forgotten what it was like to be young, innovative, and influential.

Rather than embracing the idea of a changing beat, they're lamenting the fact they can't stop it.

Perhaps the Boomers believe they have mellowed with age, abandoned their reckless behaviors in order to seriously pursue their careers and support their associations, and they're waiting for the other generations to do the same.

Undoubtedly every generation mellows as it ages, abandoning some of its risky, reckless, or immature behaviors. But one defining behavior has remained with the generations that have followed the Boomers: less membership.

As was noted a couple pages back, membership has declined about 6 percent since 1994, and much of that decline has been attributed to generational differences. This means Gen X, the oldest of who are nearing the age of 50, and now Gen Y aren't engaging in associations as much as the Baby Boomers.

On the other hand, the Millennial Impact Report by Philanthropy.com surveyed 6,522 Americans under the age of 35 and found 75 percent of survey participants donated to causes in 2013 and 63 percent gave their time to volunteer. Numerous studies support similar findings, that young people are actively involved in causes—so why not membership?

This leads me to believe two things are happening:

1. The Boomers have, perhaps unknowingly, created organizations of exclusivity rather than inclusion. These organizations are based on traditions and cater to the needs, values, and interests of Boomers. As a result, younger generations don't feel they belong and therefore don't feel compelled to participate; and

2. There are real and significant differences in what inspires younger generations to join, engage, lead, and volunteer. Membership is not something you get serious about or grow into once you hit 40. That theory is flawed; and it's also giving associations a false sense of security.

Associations must evolve, and they must do so at the same pace as the rest of society. If they can't keep up, don't define the future, and ignore the changing demographics, associations risk becoming obsolete. That's not an empty threat. It's already happening and it's about to accelerate.

While declining engagement among younger generations has been a recognized and researched trend for the past 10 years and even longer, the severity of the situation is gaining momentum as the largest generation in history moves into adulthood.

It's one thing to not be able to engage Generation X, which is a small generation (48 million Americans) in comparison to the Boomers

(78 million Americans). But that's nothing compared to the challenge that lies before us now.

Simply put, if your association can't engage the largest population in the world, your association will probably cease to exist.

Generation Y

Dear readers, please allow me to introduce you to Generation Y (1982–1995). Believe me when I say that knowing Y and what inspires them to join and engage, will be the difference between your association's success and demise.

Generation Y, also known as Millennials, are the children of the Baby Boomers. In fact, at 80 million Americans they outnumber the Boomer generation. According to the U.S. Census Bureau, by 2015 Baby Boomers will cede the majority of the workforce to Generation Y, marking the largest shift in human capital in history.

In 2015, when this generation becomes the majority workforce, they will be between the ages of 20 and 33. This means the majority of our workforce will be 20-something years old.

This demographic poses a great threat—and opportunity—to nearly every industry sector, government entity, nonprofit, and membership association, which are still managed, governed, and supported almost entirely by Baby Boomers.

According to the U.S. Census Bureau, 10,000 Boomers will retire everyday for the next 15 years in the United States alone. This demographic shift is mirrored in developed nations throughout the world. In Australia, there are 6 million Gen Ys in comparison to 5 million Boomers. Gen Y in India is a whopping 426 million (six times larger than the United States) and in China 218 million Gen Ys were born in a single decade (1980–1990).

Associations are ill prepared for this shift. The arrival of the Y generation will be revolutionary for associations, much like the arrival of the Boomer generation revolutionized the world. In that regard, history is repeating itself. However, the arrival of Gen Y isn't just about a young demographic coming into power. It's not just their age that defines this generation, nor their size that makes them capable of revolution. This generation is actually introducing an entirely new value system to the marketplace. Often dismissed as entitled, self-centered, attention-deficit, immature, and incapable of interpersonal communication, few leaders and organizations have taken the extra step to delve into what motivates and inspires Generation Y and influences their decision to engage.

Think you know Y? Think again.

This tech-savvy, globally minded generation isn't joining, buying, networking, learning, or engaging like other generations. This generation has been difficult to engage because the traditional membership doesn't meet their values and therefore falls drastically short of meeting their expectations.

For example, this generation:

• Hates to be sold anything;

• Has always been rewarded for participation and not achievement;

• Doesn't seek to acquire stuff—including association memberships;

• Can self-organize friends for grassroots activism;

• Trusts peers first and parents second;

• Actively researches prices and reads reviews before making a purchase;

• Is driven by a desire to make a difference;

• Expects exceptional service, like Amazon.com which suggests products they might like;

• Seeks to do business with ethical, trustworthy organizations;

• Values customization, customizing everything from their music to shoes and M&Ms; and

• Remains detached from institutions but closely networked with friends.

Further exploration of Generation Y's shifting values reveals that as this generation has aged, many of the cornerstones of associations have lost their value and become irrelevant.

Here's a snapshot of some of the most dramatic shifts, and some of the comments Generation Y made about each:

• **Ownership versus Access**
    After defining ourselves for centuries by possessions—cars, houses, books, china patterns, stocks, boats, land, and jewelry—what matters to a growing number of young people is not so much ownership as access. The pressure is on for associations to deliver continued, quick, and easy access to new information, valuable services and products, meaningful relationships, and experiences that deliver a real return on investment. In fact, associations may need to move away from the

concepts of joining and investing in a year-round membership, both of which are ownership traits.

> *"My generation is looking to make a difference. Anytime we send in our dues, it's to make a difference and because we believe in the cause. We may not be joiners but we are supporters. That's probably a change in mindset from other generations. It means we want to support and serve the association as long as we can make a difference with our peers and community."*

Chris Beaman
Assistant Director of Membership & Chapter Services
Kappa Delta Pi
Age: 25

• Loyalty versus Relationships

Generation Y is more apt to move from one opportunity to the next, garnering them a reputation for having a lack of loyalty. It's not that younger professionals don't embody loyalty. Gen Ys are very loyal—they're just not loyal to institutions; they are loyal to people. Effective and inspirational leaders or mentors are frequently cited as the primary reason Gen Y will first engage with an organization. Gen Y commits when meaningful relationships and great experiences are actively present. To them, loyalty is not something you do just because; it is something that is earned.

> *"I'm engaged because being engaged has given me a high profile in my industry and the association. Being engaged gave me the opportunity to learn new skills and find new talent for my team. I've seen people get jobs and move up. I've made great contacts that I'll have for my lifetime. I tell people this is the greatest investment in yourself that you'll ever make."*

Jonathan McGrew
Co-Chair, Young Professionals Group
Business Marketing Association Colorado
Age: 29

• Community versus Globalization

Members of the older generations are more likely to define community as knowing your neighbors and participating in an association's events. Generation Y thinks of community as having access to and interacting with a global network via social media. Globalization is something earlier generations could only consider in abstract terms; Generation Y has always lived it. As a result, some

Gen Ys are pushing back on the concept of associations having chapters, not seeing the need to be organized by geography and desiring the option to be organized by common interests instead.

> *"I think associations need to assess whether geographic structures matter. The chapter structure seems a bit dated and stodgy. If it's working for your association, then keep doing it, but individuals should be able to strike out on their own and start affinity groups based on common interests. I think my generation wants the opportunity to define ourselves rather than be defined by the association based on where we live."*
>
> Michael Nevergall
> Associate Vice President
> Development Lutheran Social Services of the South
> Age: 31

- ## Advocacy versus Social Awareness
While the majority of this generation showed up at the polls in the last two elections, they aren't especially politically savvy. This is partly due to decreasing civics curriculum in schools during the past two decades. However, Gen Ys are very socially aware and frequently cite improving education, ending poverty, and saving the environment as their top concerns. They are more likely to buy products that support sustainable farming or fair trade, and 85 percent link commitment to a cause to their purchasing decisions. Gen Y doesn't believe advocacy is something they can positively influence. Associations will need to reconsider their approach, likely by educating, empowering, and engaging Gen Y in grassroots advocacy.

> *"There's a big disconnect in my generation with lobbying and government. I didn't know what grassroots and lobbying were until I started working with associations. I voted because that's what everyone does—that's what we are supposed to do—but policies and proposed bills, I admit, I haven't paid much attention to. Honestly, I'm so disconnected politically—and I think that's true for most people in my generation—that I don't know what policies are in place. So if your association is trying to tell me it's beneficial to get involved to change policy, I'm not going to understand or value that change. Most advocacy efforts are not going to make any difference to me until or unless I understand the policies in place."*
>
> Megan Shankle
> Account Executive, ISG Solutions
> Age: 32

- **Status versus Inclusion**

  Leadership is not synonymous with years of experience. No longer is all the wisdom and experience contained within the eldest, predominantly white, male population. This hierarchical, homogenous model survived for centuries, but it is no longer relevant or sustainable. Generation Y is the most racially and ethnically diverse generation in history, the most tech-savvy and entrepreneurial, the most educated, and the first to have more women than men obtain postsecondary credentials. In the corporate world, there is ample evidence that companies with inclusive, diverse leadership are considerably more profitable than companies with homogenous leadership. Associations need to take note and reformat their boards of directors to allow for the participation of members from all ages and backgrounds.

  > *"Young professionals won't come to an event that's traditional, stodgy, and scary and hang out with a bunch of old white guys in suits. Associations must have the ability to adapt and let new ideas—and people—come to the table."*
  >
  > Ashley Hodak Sullivan
  > Chief Operating Officer
  > New York State Trial Lawyers Association
  > Age: 28

- **Jobs versus Entrepreneurs**

  It used to be that you would choose a career, get a job, and work for that industry—sometimes for the same company—until you retired. In recent years, we've seen the emergence of the Gig Economy in which more workers detach from conventional jobs to take on contract work and other short-term gigs. Add to that the widespread demand for flextime, increased demands for skilled labor, Gen Y's desire to quickly move up or across, and the fact that Ys have launched a record numbers of start-up businesses, one can quickly surmise that the world of work isn't about working 9 to 5 anymore. The entire workforce is moving into an entrepreneurial mindset both figuratively and literally. This is likely to require associations to reconsider their member benefits as well as the length of membership. After all, if you juggle responsibilities or change jobs every year or so, you may not have enough time or affinity for a profession to want to join an association.

"I feel really busy. I work long days—sometimes 12 hours. I also volunteer at church and sit on my college alumni council. What personal time I have, I spend with my family or friends. So if I'm making time to squeeze in one more thing, it had better be good."

Young Professional
Assistant Project Manager
Age: 27

• Sales versus Service

Associations spend a considerable amount of time and resources on membership recruitment—or sales. Generation Y, on the other hand, is turned off by anything resembling a sales pitch. They would rather establish a meaningful relationship and the only way to get there is by providing exceptional service. Ys want personalized, knowledgeable human interaction when they interact with your association. They want to see that the association is connected and responsive to their specific needs. They want to feel appreciated, valuable, and important. Ys are very smart, savvy consumers and they will do their homework before they purchase anything. Ys will want facts about your association. Crystal-clear, no frills communication that helps them understand how your association makes a difference in their lives and the lives of others is key. This will likely mean associations will need to shift their focus from sales to service; recruitment to relationship-building. Because when it comes to selling memberships—it's really not about selling at all.

"You have one, maybe two chances with my generation before you burn the bridge. You have to make it easy to find information on the association and its events. You almost have to spoon-feed us information. The more information we can access and the easier you make the whole engagement process, the more likely you will get my generation engaged."

Jenny Matthews
Executive Director
Tennessee Society of Association Executives
Age: 30

• Control versus Freedom

Associations were founded on the premise that certain rules needed to be followed (bylaws) and traditions upheld. Year in and year out, the association provided the same products, services, events, and member benefits. Members could pay their dues literally and figuratively, eventually gaining enough experience to sit on a committee or the board of directors. This fostered more of a command-control, industrial environment—everything ran according to expectations, process, and hierarchy. This left little room for innovation or change. However, there's been more technology developed in the last five years than the last 50 years. From a technology perspective alone, we can conclude that associations have to forego operating in a controlled environment and be open to new ideas emerging everywhere, from everyone.

> *"I always appreciate thinking outside of the box, and as a leader I insist we change things up, even if they're working. I'm always asking 'Can we do this better?' and I'm always recruiting new people because I know they will bring new ideas and experiences to the table. In the future, the most successful organizations will be open to change and never comfortable with the status quo."*
>
> Justin Wutzke
> National Board of Directors, U.S. Jaycees
> Chair of the Board, Montana Jaycees
> Age: 31

Critical to that last point is the fact that associations will be challenged to innovate not just a little bit or once, but significantly and diligently, without pause. More than 100 Gen Ys were surveyed and interviewed in the process of researching this book and the relentless pursuit of innovation was a common theme throughout the responses.

Relentless Pursuit of Innovation

"We're moving into something drastically different than what we're used to. Traditional thinking doesn't work with this generation. It's viewed as old school and turns them off," explained Mark Koepsell, CAE and CEO of Synergos, an association management company that manages the Association of Fraternity/Sorority Advisors and the Association of Fraternal Leadership & Values.

Koepsell has worked in higher education for 17 years, moving into association management in 2009. He cautions that associations are very accustomed to doing things the way they've always been done, yet Generation Y has a seemingly insatiable desire to do what's different and new. "The most difficult part of working with Generation Y is that you can't just push "repeat." In managing our associations, which serve college students, we are always innovating and improving because this generation doesn't want more of the same."

Knowing how to engage Generation Y begins with knowing why this generation is unlike any other. It's equally important to know why engaging this generation will be the best business decision your association will make. Take note: The behaviors and choices of younger generations have historically been an indicator of future workplace, consumer, and economic trends.

MEMBERSHIP OUTSIDE THE UNITED STATES

What's happening to membership outside of the United States? Membership is healthy, but there are definitely red flags popping up all over the world.

United Kingdom

For the U.K. associations responding to the *2013–14 Membership Benchmarking Report,* authored by Sue Froggatt, 71 percent expect membership to grow. However, recruiting members, engaging members, retaining existing members, and attracting younger members were all ranked as the most challenging endeavors.

Canada

Associations in Canada have consistently identified growth and retention as top priorities. According to the 2013 *Pulse Report* distributed by Greenfield Services, 33.1 percent of associations reported growth in membership and 48.4 percent report stable membership numbers in 2013. These stats are virtually unchanged compared to 2012.

However, Meagan Rockett, director of client services at Greenfield Services, noted efforts to engage the next generation of members was trending downward. Reportedly, 34.7 percent of the associations said they were working on a plan to engage Generation Y in 2012, versus 26 percent in 2013.

"My opinion is that the decision-makers and top-level executives are predominantly Boomers still and don't quite know how, or how to start, to attract and communicate with the next generation of member and leader," Rockett said.

Holland

Associations in Holland are experiencing widespread change. Previously, associations were intertwined with government, with patient-associations serving patients of diseases receiving 90 percent of their budgets from government subsidies. Furthermore, businesses were required by law to join a chamber of commerce. Now these entities have been totally reorganized because the political climate no longer supports these obligations for businesses, and government funding for patient associations has ceased.

continued on next page

The same is true for membership right now. The trends and influences introduced and shaped by Generation Y are having a Trickle-Up Effect— changing the value of membership and expectations of the membership experience for every generation. Trickle-Up Effect, also known as "bubble-up effect," is a term that has been used to describe the flow of wealth and fashion trends. In both cases, as in this case, movement is from the bottom up and eventually influences the majority. In other words, if membership

---

continued from previous page

Jeanne Hoogers, editor of *VM,* an association management magazine, explains that Holland is moving from being an over-organized society in addition to managing the changes associated with globalization, technology, economic crisis, and demographic shifts. "The climate changes are in some ways the same as in the United States, but we are a small, very urbanized country so the effect is stronger," she explained. Membership in professional associations remains healthy, but Holland is concerned about high unemployment among its young people and there are the same concerns about staying relevant to this generation. "Associations find that they have to appeal to younger generations, but also have to rethink the future: What are our members going through? What are the major changes in their environment, what is our possible contribution and role?"

Hoogers said her personal observation is that many associations don't want to make mistakes, and don't really want to share the responsibility of creating the future with the members. "We are in the middle of some major changes—a period of transition—so associations have to be/become extremely flexible and agile. They really need to focus on what their members and not-yet members or not-anymore members want, experience, like, search for, want to share. If they focus too much on the future of the association as it is now, they will leave a lot of room for new, competitive ways of organizing."

Australia

According to the *Associations Matter: 2013 State of the Sector Study*—a lengthy study of 23 associations and 7,749 members conducted by Survey Matters—92 percent of respondents expect the demand for professional associations to remain stable or increase.

This finding was tempered by the comments shared by Survey Matters' researchers in the findings report: "No longer just providers of member services and discounts, associations need to look to the practices of leading digital publishing houses, educational institutions and marketing agencies. They need to cultivate their reputation as the authoritative source of knowledge, with access to the most up to date and trusted sources of information and training in the industry. If associations are going to recruit, engage and retain members in the future, they must adapt and evolve. They must keep up."

is declining in value for Generation Y, soon it will decline in value for *all* generations.

This would seem like "The End of Membership as We Know It"—but it actually marks the beginning of unparalleled opportunity for those associations willing to embrace change and innovate. Like the Air Traffic Controllers Association, which shifted its focus onto Generation Y in 2011, resulting in a 30 percent membership increase and 25 percent increase in event attendance of all generations of members. Equally impressive, the association's bottom line emerged from losing $300,000 per year to establishing a healthy and growing financial reserve. Or the Marine Retailers Association of the Americas, which launched a Young Leaders Advisory Council in 2009, and observed a 200 percent membership increase and $100,000 revenue increase.

These are two examples of the Trickle-Up Effect at work. Focusing on the successful engagement of a Generation Y membership significantly improved engagement and revenue for the entire membership. Now you have a choice. You can choose to dwell on the challenges that lie ahead and the unprecedented and significant shifts leading to irrelevance, or you can dwell on the opportunities and create something of unprecedented and significant relevance. You can lament the potential loss of a disengaged future majority, or you can envision the potential impact of an engaged future majority. You can choose to believe that stopping the beat is an impossible feat, or you can move your membership to a new beat. But one thing is certain—whatever choice you make from here on out, it will begin and end with Y.

CHAPTER 2

Mission Possible

"Now members own the relationship with associations. This is a shift. It used to be associations owned the relationship."

Chris Beaman
Assistant Director of Membership and Chapter
Services
Kappa Delta Pi
Age: 25

Harley-Davidson is a true American icon with real brand cachet. For a particular breed of leather wearing motorcycle enthusiasts, there is simply nothing on par with Harley. The motorcycle company was founded in 1901, but it wasn't until the arrival of the Baby Boomers that the brand really blossomed and sales skyrocketed. Boomers embraced the Harley bikes as totems of rebellion in the 1960s and 1970s and drove its growth in the ensuing decades.

This is just one example of a brand that benefitted from the arrival of the Boomer generation. As one of the wealthiest generations in history, the Boomers had a vast influence on the economy. They were one of the first generations to really grab the attention of the marketing and advertising world as retailers and savvy businesses realized that young Americans could be an indicator of future trends and a key cog in the economic engine that drives consumerism in America.

Youth. It's why Harley thrived under the Boomer youth regime, Nike thrived under the Gen X youth regime, and Apple is thriving under the Gen Y regime.However, Harley has made headlines in national media recently, as motorcycle sales seem to be in decline. *Forbes* reports Harley observed a unit decrease of nearly 30 percent within six years. As one *Forbes* columnist wrote, "Harley will never get its old mojo back for one critical reason that is completely outside of its control: demographics."

Harley Davidson's brand and sales depend disproportionately—almost exclusively, in fact—on middle-aged Caucasian males. In recent years the company has tried to expand its reach to women, minorities, and younger generations with limited success. Perhaps Harley Davidson waited too long to engage other demographics, riding on the success of the Boomers and never really thinking about the future. Perhaps the passing of the Harley era is a reminder that different generations have different interests, and not everything that was relevant to one generation will be relevant to the next. Perhaps it's a little of both.

Associations need to be careful not to follow suit. Paying close attention to the changing needs and values of the marketplace is critical. This is especially apparent with the arrival of Generation Y.

Unlike their Baby Boomer parents, Gen Y isn't the wealthiest generation, but they are the largest generation in history. Not surprising, companies of all sizes and industries are turning their attention to this gigantic and influential group of consumers, which will become the majority of the workforce by 2015.

While organizations may have first thought about Generation Y and dreamed of dollar signs, it quickly became clear this wasn't going to be an easy sell. Gen Y's buying habits are noticeably different from the generations that have come before them. Moreover, Ys perceive value and expect to receive value in very different ways.

As the first generation to be raised with access to technology, Generation Y has become known as the instant-gratification, review-driven, social-networked generation that hates to be sold anything. This generation spends a whopping $200 billion annually yet ignores advertising, which has puzzled marketers and business owners the world over.

What does the arrival of such a large and unique generation mean for the future of associations? It means the membership value proposition has to change. The Boomers are on their way out, Generation X is a small population by comparison, and Generation Y resembles the largest demographic in the world. There's no getting around it. Your association needs the participation of Gen Y in order to survive.

Plus, as I mentioned in Chapter 1, Generation Y is redefining value for everyone. Their unique interests, needs, and values heavily influence their decisions to engage—and these behaviors have begun to influence the way every generation engages. It's a Trickle-Up Effect. Generation Y could change membership the same way Boomers changed the motorcycle industry. The only difference is the motorcycle industry embraced the new generation of consumers (Boomers), and for the most part associations haven't exactly embraced the new generation of members (Generation Y) much beyond the launch of young professional groups.

The value of membership has shifted and if they don't respond to the shift, associations, also like motorcycles, will become under-utilized, irrelevant, thereby experiencing revenue loss and aging out. Change is possible. It's just a matter of finding what's valuable and moving towards it. Consumer trends are an excellent place to start.

Recessionistas and Migrators

Generation Y is turning out to be radically different than any other generation out there. For starters, their buying behaviors are unique. Their arrival has confounded many retailers because they are well-informed consumers who walk into stores knowing a great deal about the product; thrifty consumers who tend to reuse and recycle; and investment consumers willing to pay more for quality and trendy brands.

For Ys, it's the trifecta of quality, popularity, and price that drives sales. However, Ys will make the occasional concession if two out of three of their criteria are met. For example, UGG boots come with a price tag starting at $135—a bit steep for a new college grad or entry-level professional—but Gen Y pays for the boots because they have been popular for several years and are renowned with high quality.

On the other hand, Gen Y will search for competitive prices on Amazon, linger over the best deals at a discount store, and then sell their used goods on Craigslist. Part of this stems from their experience of coming of age during a recession. Having incurred the largest credit card and college debt of any other generation, faced the highest jobless rate since the Great Depression, and trademarked the "Boomerang Generation" for moving back in with their parents, Ys have had to scale back on reaching major milestones and hunker down with reality. As such, this generation has been dubbed "Recessionistas"—informed shoppers who stick to tight budgets while still managing to stay trendy and cultured.

Associations need to understand the financial situation of Gen Y. While they occasionally splurge, the fact is that the largest generation in history might never spend as lavishly as its parents did. For some associations, the price of membership will hinder Gen Y's ability to join.

In addition to taking an association's quality, popularity, and price under advisement, associations can expect Gen Y to also apply their migratory interests to assess whether a membership is the best fit for them.

Just after the close of World War II, a migration in the United States took place. Large numbers of people moved from the city to the new suburbs fueled by new roads, low congestion, and modest energy costs. It was a new beginning for Baby Boomers and the American Dream became synonymous with obtaining a big house, sprawling lawn, and white picket fence.

After that, it didn't take long for the preferred retailers and businesses to do likewise, abandoning the city and following their customers to the suburbs. Commercial buildings and large indoor shopping malls were built.

Now, Generation Y is moving back into cities, leading what's been referred to as the Great Migration of the 21st Century. According to RCLCO, research analysts specializing in the real estate industry, 77 percent of Generation Y will live in an urban core and influence widespread urban revitalization until 2050.

Generation Y is literally migrating away from the interests and behaviors of their predecessors and the influences of their childhood. These migrations are great indicators to the types of value propositions that will motivate and appeal to Generation Y.

- **Safety to Adventure**

  Generation Y has grown up in the safest environment in human history. The suburban cul-de-sac offered a safe place to play, with lower crime rates than cities. But despite this safe environment, the need to fill a 24-hour news cycle in the emerging world of cable and online communications brought every localized "stranger danger" news story to a national audience, giving rise to the overprotective Helicopter Parents (Boomers) who watched over every minute of their children's (Gen Y) lives.

  As young adults, this over-protected generation is migrating from safety to adventure. They seek frequent opportunities to travel and dangerous and exciting sports activities like skydiving, rock climbing, and bungee jumping.

  The equivalent of this trend in the association world is innovation and a willingness to take risks or end the rules. I know of an association that about six years ago finally changed language in their bylaws referring to notifying members by telegraph! This association certainly wouldn't pass Gen Y's adventure criteria.

  "Much of my client base is just now catching up to social media and using it as a way to reach and service their membership. I've used social media for several years now. Because associations tend to be a step behind in their use of technology, they tend not to be as enticing to my generation," explained Megan Shankle, a Gen Y who works for ISG Solutions, an association management software provider for associations and nonprofits. Even though ISG has developed technology that provides dashboarding to make data easier to understand, Shankle said some association leaders she meets with "fear change" and the idea of "letting technology take over." It's this safe zone that prohibits innovation, efficiency, and turns her generation off, Shankle explained.

Although he's not a Gen Y, Byron Patrick does hold the honor of being one of the youngest board chairs for the Maryland Association of CPAs. When the 36 year old was named chair, he celebrated by getting a large tattoo on his forearm bearing the CPA symbol. When he showed the tattoo to a group of former board chairs, whom he described as "much older," he recalls "they looked at me like I had four heads."

Younger generations want an opportunity to break the mold and try new things and they want their organizations to be cutting-edge, or at least appreciate a cutting-edge mindset. Too much resistance to innovation, technology, or change will put your association in the safe zone, the very place Ys are trying to escape.

- **Isolated to Connected**
  While the suburban cul-de-sac lifestyle offered a safe environment, it also produced an isolated and disconnected environment. Today's children rarely have the freedom to roam beyond the cul-de-sac, ensuring their social lives are determined by the quality of friends on the same street, together with the nature of their scheduled social interactions beyond their neighborhood.

  As young adults, Generation Y wants to be more connected and less isolated. They manifest this desire in their full-on embrace of social media and their desire to live in places where they can be around others—including the densest, most active areas of cities.

  Associations can fulfill their desire for connectivity through communication and by providing ways for members to interact with one another. In surveys and interviews with Generation Y, many complained they are not well informed or don't understand how to quickly get involved in an association and start meeting people.

  Alexa Anason, 27, is actively involved in a few associations and was previously involved in another. She attests her generation is not difficult to engage in associations, as long as the association excels at making a connection with them, which starts with technology. "I've noticed that associations can be slow to move on things, especially technology. Technology is extremely important to my generation. I want to access information about the association and content relevant to my industry through the association's blogs, social media pages, and any other relevant outlets available."

She added that some associations are, at times, not the best at promoting their networks—an area of connectivity and value to Generation Y. "My generation wants to network with people who can help us build our careers. It would be great if associations could draw more attention to the member companies involved so we know who we're likely to meet and that the networking will be beneficial for us."

However, Anason points out that connectivity isn't just about technology or networking; it's also how members are valued. "I've attended some association events that I could have joined but I didn't. Those experiences were somewhat cold and I didn't have as many conversations with people because everyone already knew each other and only wanted to stick with their clique. I don't want to be part of an association, or any group for that matter, that is like that."

do we have cliques?

The most networked, educated, tech-savvy generation sees associations as an opportunity to further their online and in-person connectivity efforts, potentially leading them to career opportunities, skills, industry information, and relationships.

- **Inconvenient to Convenient**

Convenience is another word for time, and Generation Y has a low tolerance for spending time on things associated with the suburban lifestyle, such as yard work or long commutes in the car. Instead, they want the convenience of living close to the things they need and the things they do.

To Gen Y, a car is no longer a convenience if it's a 20-minute trip to buy a quart of milk. This generation has grown up with the world at their fingertips, able to communicate within seconds around the world via technology. As such, they are programmed to get things instantly. Convenience really matters to Generation Y, and should be a priority consideration when interacting with this generation.

At 30, Jenny Matthews is one of the youngest executive directors of a state society of association executives in the nation. She was recently appointed executive director of the Tennessee Society of Association Executives and she feels strongly about creating a convenience factor within associations.

"You have one, maybe two chances with my generation before you burn the bridge. You have to make it easy to find information on the association and its events," she explained. "You almost have to spoon-feed us information. The more information we can access and the

easier you make the whole engagement process, the more likely you
will get my generation engaged."

Clearly, Ys are informed, selective consumers (Recessionistas). They
are drawn to innovation, connectivity, and convenience (Migrators). They
research every company they come into contact with, and they will do the
same with your association.

Expect them to peruse the association's home page, and if that holds
their interest, they will likely seek out information on engagement
opportunities, high-profile members, member benefits, videos about the
association, and media mentions.

The chart below demonstrates the core interests of Generation Y,
as developed by the Recessionista and Migrator influences, and the
questions they are likely to want answered upon an initial search of your
association's website.

RECESSIONISTAS	MIGRATORS
Quality *Are there ample opportunities to further my career?*	**Adventure** *Does this association appear to be innovative, progressive, and open to change?*
Popularity *Is the association reputable, well known, and a leader in its industry?*	**Connected** *Does this association have an active social media presence and ways for me to easily and quickly meet other members?*
Price *Does the membership offer a significant return on investment?*	**Convenient** *Is the website experience easy, informative, and intuitive?*

But the Recessionista and Migrator mindsets are just the tip of the
iceberg. Generation Y's value system is also influenced by the concepts
of Access and Sharing—two additional factors positioned to dramatically
change the future of associations.

Access and Sharing

After defining ourselves for generations by possessions—cars, houses,
books, china patterns, stocks, boats, land, and jewelry—a dramatic shift
is under way. In the wake of a collapsed economy and a warming planet,
what matters to a growing number of young people is not so much
ownership as access.

Times are tough. For the first time, the rising generation is genuinely concerned that their standard of living will be worse than it was for the generation that came before them. (That's saying a lot considering Generation X has lived through four recessions and is renowned for being the most debt-ridden generation in history.)

Simultaneously, technology is enabling a new kind of connectedness and sharing, more Gen Ys than any other generation are moving to urban areas, and there's an increased awareness about harmful climate change. As a result, Gen Y is starting to rethink what it means to own something. In turn, that's giving rise to the emergence of the Sharing Economy, which thrives on the process of sharing products and services to mutually make each other's lives easier/happier/better.

More than a century ago consumption began to emerge as a driving force and curator in American life. By the time the 1950s rolled around (when Boomers were being born) families started moving to the suburbs, accumulated possessions like new appliances, bigger cars, and fancier houses, and tried to keep up with "The Jones." Then businesses began rolling out new versions of products that were somehow always better, faster, and smarter than the ones that had come before. The psychological effects were powerful, and they're still with us today—as anybody who has seen, or stood in, the lines outside of an Apple store before the release of a new iPhone can attest.

After a century of working ever harder to own more, Generation Y seems to be stopping that ingrained societal cycle and changing the concept of ownership. They are open to the idea of sharing more and owning less.

It's no coincidence that Facebook has a "Share" button. Generation Y loves sharing information via social media, but the Sharing Economy moves way beyond technology. For example, Generation Y is the primary user of Zipcar, the world's largest car sharing program providing car reservations billable by the hour or the day. Interesting enough, Zipcar is a membership program, completely based on the principles of the Sharing Economy (also known as the Peer Economy) and Gen Y's interest in access rather than ownership. For $6 per month members can reserve Zipcars online or by phone, immediately or up to a year in advance. Members have automated access to Zipcars using an access card, which works with the car's technology to unlock the door, where the keys are already located inside. Zipcar also offers an app that allows members to honk the horn to locate a Zipcar and unlock the doors. Driving rates range from $8–$10 per hour. Gas, parking, insurance, and maintenance are included in the price. As of July 2013, Zipcar had 810,000 members—up 50,000 from 2008.

Airbnb is another prominent example of the Sharing Economy, in which people rent beds, cars, boats and other assets directly from each other, coordinated via the internet. Dubbed the world's largest community hospitality company, Airbnb is a website for people to list and rent out lodging, including private rooms, entire apartments, castles, boats, manors, tree houses, tipis, igloos, private islands, and other properties. It has over 500,000 listings in 33,000 cities and 192 countries. In 2012 alone, more than 2.5 million people used the site.

Other pioneers of the Sharing Economy, providing goods and services to others for a rental fee, are SnapGoods (high-end household goods), DogVacay (dog sitters), TaskRabbit (personal assistants), Liquid (bicycles), and Fon (Wi-Fi access).

Some of this sharing, of course, is a result of the economic downturn. But that's not the whole story. Craigslist and eBay both launched in 1995, allowing people to buy and sell goods from one another. So it's not just an outcome of the recession. There's been a shift in mindset as well, and Generation Y was born and raised amidst this new sharing era. As a result, Generation Y is increasingly forgoing the hassles of ownership. What they care most about is not ownership but access.

This shift is evident in the resurgence in urban redevelopment in urban centers all over the world. Urban redevelopment is occurring, in large part, because Generation Y isn't migrating to the suburbs as young adults to begin their ownership and accumulation process. Gen Ys want to stay in close proximity to where they live, work, and do business, and they value that convenience more than the ownership of land, houses, and stuff in general.

The only caveat being, of course, is the ownership of technology. Yes, this generation will invest in technology and they want their smartphones and laptops and tablets in close proximity at all times. But keep in mind that even the accumulation of technology isn't as much about ownership as it is about access. Technology gives them access—quick and easy access—to information, relationships, shopping, entertainment, and nearly all the essentials and tasks affiliated with everyday life.

What does this mean for membership? It means the days of buying a membership and holding onto that membership for several years, even decades, is over.

Think about it. When you join or renew your membership, you are basically signing a contract with that association for the next year. You are paying in advance, assuring your loyalty and contribution, and in exchange you are given a membership. It can be argued that you are purchasing access when you buy a membership, but you are paying whether you utilize the association or not. It's similar to buying a car. You buy the car and you continue to make the payments—even if it sat all year in the garage—because you own it. It's the same with membership. Joining an association because it's the right thing to do is an ownership behavior. Renewing a membership even if you only attended one event last year is an ownership behavior.

Associations can no longer think of themselves as an entity that people join and take great pride in referring to themselves as members, even going so far as to hang up plaques and window decals to announce their membership. That's an ownership behavior.

Associations must now shift their expectations and think in terms of access. The pressure is on for associations to deliver continued, quick, and easy access to new information, valuable services and products, meaningful relationships, and experiences that deliver a real return on investment.

The Boomers tend to criticize younger generations as not being joiners, but I don't think that's an accurate assessment. It would be more accurate to say Gen Ys aren't owners. This generation isn't driven to own a membership, just as they aren't driven to buy land, houses, cars, and jewelry. Rather, they seek to access great resources through engagement.

In other words, associations have to start thinking less about getting people to join the association, and more about what they offer that is truly engaging. Focus less on driving ownership and more on providing access.

Clearly, the emergence of the Sharing Economy plays a role in Gen Y's expectations, too. Associations tend to think of the membership experience as something that an individual pursues and something that's propelled by individual behaviors: pay your dues, volunteer your time, take your time off work to attend an event, and so forth. Yet, the Sharing Economy isn't propelled by the concept of an individual serving an association. The Sharing Economy thrives on the process of sharing products and services to mutually make each other's lives easier/happier/ better.

Furthermore, while Gen Y is often criticized for being entitled and incapable of relationship building, the Sharing Economy is entirely based on collaborative and community-building concepts! It's simply a different approach than what society is used to in both regards. We used to borrow cups of sugar from the neighbors and tools from close friends, but Gen Y is sharing all kinds of products and services with an entire network of total strangers.

Not only that, but by entering into this sharing agreement, there's a positive shared outcome, such as reducing environmental impact, reducing overhead and costs, building communities, utilizing previously under-utilized resources, and generating a positive economic climate. In essence, sharing opens the door to giving.

It's radical to think of associations as a place where sharing frequently occurs, allowing for greater access and outcomes for the betterment of all involved. Yes, associations foster the sharing of knowledge and business cards, but the Sharing Economy opens the door to all types of new opportunities for associations.

Consider the operational benefits of participating in the Sharing Economy by renting out underused assets within the association itself, like office space and meeting rooms. Better yet, create an online sharing board on your association's website and allow members to share products, services, and office space with one another. Most businesses at one point *Web* or another need temporary help or technology services. Create a platform *Page* where members could post openings and hire help on a project basis. Or simply design products to be more sharable and easier to access. Zipcar developed a wireless entry mechanism so members could rent their vehicles without needing to pick up or hand off car keys. The point is to identify areas of inconvenience and hassle and resolve them for your members.

Associations will need to evolve from the "individual-must-serve-the-association" approach to membership, and instead focus on ways to generate collaboration and sharing for the purpose of building a sharing community and making the lives of members' easier/happier/better.

Membership Value Proposition

When companies hit tough times, they usually take a look at the performance and health of the business, brand, strategy, market motivators and values, and consider what and how it needs to change. Your association needs to do the same.

Aging membership, decreasing engagement among young people, and changing values have been emerging over the last several years and certainly will not diminish at any point in the near future. Associations that ignore these trends will create problems for themselves by neglecting their external and internal images as they relate to future members, employees, and leaders.

Throughout history we've seen examples of how younger generations tend to change the habits and mindsets of entire populations. This is the Trickle-Up Effect I referred to previously. Here are three examples of the Trickle-Up Effect:

1. The 1969 movie, *Easy Rider,* was a turning point for Harley Davidson motorcycles. Up until that time, Harley's motorcycles had primarily been used in combat service during World War I and World War II and for racing enthusiasts. Sales were faltering and then a character named Captain America with a flag-covered bike came along. The *Easy Rider* plot focused on a Harley cross-country ride taken by two biker-hippies. The movie became renowned as a generational icon for the Boomers, highlighting the sociological changes taking place in western society at that time. Suddenly motorcycles represented rebellion, freedom—a lifestyle based on the values Boomers coveted and wanted to emulate in their daily lives.

   Boomers started the motorcycle wave and motorcycle sales overall quickly began to trickle-up. In 1973, motorcycle sales overall hit an all-time high of 1.5 million and by the mid-80s, the fastest growing group of motorcycle owners were ages 45 to 64—the Silent Generation (1927 and 1945).

2. When Generation X moved into the workforce, they introduced the concept of working remotely and flextime. In the late 1990s I was working for an association. My manager (a Boomer) and I (an Xer) were interviewing marketing companies for a project, and I'll never forget what happened when one of the candidates (an Xer) told us her marketing company was virtual and all her employees worked remotely. I was comfortable with the idea, but when I looked over at my boss, she was visibly confused and stunned by this CEO's description of her company.

   She abruptly ended the interview, shut the door to her office, and ranted—arms flying in the air: "That's ridiculous to think you could work on projects and manage people without being in the same office! What is she thinking? I can't imagine why she would think we'd take her seriously. That's not even a business for goodness sakes!"

   I tried to tell her that virtual and remote workplaces were the wave of the future, but she would have none of it. Ironically, two years later I started a virtual company and the association was one of my first clients. A few years after that, my former boss, who couldn't fathom the idea of working anywhere but in an office, started doing some work from home. Today, working remotely, virtually, and using flextime are popular—even mainstream—practices.

3. Mark Zuckerberg, a student at Harvard, created Facebook in 2004. The site grew rapidly, adding more college campuses and expanding globally. By the end of 2005, Facebook had 5.5 million users, all were college students. It wasn't until 2006 that the site opened to anyone ages 13 and above.

At first, Boomers took little to no interest in the Facebook concept. The social media audience was heavily skewed towards Generation Y. However, in November 2010, CBS News reported that the number of Boomers using social media had skyrocketed from one million Facebook users aged 55 and older in 2009 to 10 million in 2010. According to the report, a key driver for Boomer social media use was their desire to connect with ever-more-distant kids and grandkids that were connecting more often via social networks and avoiding the telephone.

It took six years from the time Facebook launched until it became an accepted medium for Boomers. That surge in interest has continued, and ironically Facebook is now concerned about losing market share among its younger generations.

Each of these changes started with a shift in interests, spurred by the youngest generation, which eventually trickled-up and changed the behaviors of older generations. Associations need to heed this trend. The more younger generations demand a return on investment from associations and shy away from joining, the more likely that's going to become the accepted norm for all generations in the future.

Generation Y has been the most difficult generation to engage. This is due, in large part, to a values shift that has taken place. Eventually, that value shift will begin to influence the decision-making and engagement processes of other generations, too. Ys are genuinely motivated in different ways than other generations, which is why associations have to rethink the Member Value Proposition and make it relevant to Generation Y.

Remember the book, *Good to Great* by Jim Collins? It was a huge best seller, selling more than four million copies in 35 languages. Collins used a team of researchers who studied 6,000 articles and generated more than 2,000 pages of interview transcripts during a five-year project to develop and write the book. He described seven characteristics of companies that went from good to great, one of which was: "First who, then what; get the right people on the bus, then figure out where to go."

The book was released in 2001, and at the time I think Jim Collins was right. But now, 15 years later, I think the most important decision an organization will make is how to create, deliver, and capture value.

Quickly. Organizations don't have the luxury of time to figure it out, as Collins suggested. A decision must be made.

Yes, the "who" part of Collins' equation is critically important. In Collins' case, when he referred to who to get on the bus, he was referring to talent. Undoubtedly, every association relies on great talent, be it staff, board members, or volunteers. And every association seeks to continually further engagement among its members, knowing the most active members contribute the most to the association and are least likely to get off the bus. However, it's because the "who" part that is lacking in today's organizations that I think we have to get back to putting "what" first. To build upon that even further, we also need to consider why.

Most associations have been really successful at engaging the Boomer generation but have continually struggled to engage younger generations, and I believe that's partly because their value propositions don't resonate with them. Plus, it's important to recognize that value is no longer created by the associations themselves, but by the people within. This is part of that values shift that's taking place—a move away from ownership in an organization just because it's the right thing to do.

Today, the people your association attracts believe in the values your association represents and provides, and they will drive that value even further through their leadership, participation, and promotion. However, no one will ever buy from or join an association if they don't even understand why they should pay attention or what value the association delivers to them in the first place. First identify what, then who.

A great value proposition is essential for any association hoping to clearly communicate to prospective members why it's different, better, and worth getting involved. It's a promise of the value your association can deliver to members; the most persuasive reason people should notice your association and engage.

Your association's mission statement defines your association's purpose; why you exist and whom you serve. It reminds leaders, staff, and members about what the organization does at its core. Consider this more of an internal roadmap.

In contrast, a value statement is intended for sharing. It's how you acknowledge that you know what the members need most and what the association does best to answer those needs. It supports your members' rationale for choosing to affiliate with your association, versus another association or no association at all, and also supports the public's image of the association. It should be very straightforward and easy to understand.

Above all, your association's value statement needs to resonate with Generation Y.

In fact, your association's value proposition should not be just for your association's leadership to decide. Rather, I would suggest having purposeful conversations with Generation Y members, staff, and prospective members to identify your association's most valuable offerings from their perspective.

Remember: This generation isn't interested in an association's traditional value system, and their view of your association's best selling points may be considerably different than what you're used to touting.

In addition, this exercise will also help you prioritize your association's strategic issues, linking what members need most with what your association focuses on and delivers with excellence.

Generation Y will do their initial research of your association online. Of course, there are additional factors that go into their decision to join, which will be addressed in the next several chapters. But the value proposition is your association's opportunity to make a great first impression. It should appear front and center on the home page of your website.

Based on the four shifts in consumerism outlined above, Generation Y is driven by quality, popularity, price, adventure, connectedness, convenience, access, and sharing. There's also an overarching demand to know how their engagement in something will make their lives easier, happier, better.

In the table below, you will see these values listed alongside a few examples of value propositions used by some notable organizations with a Gen Y following:

EASIER	HAPPIER	BETTER
Convenience Access Sharing	Adventure Connectedness	Quality Popularity Price
iTunes: *You've never been so easily entertained*	Red Bull: *Wings when you need them*	Kiva: *Loans that change lives*
Shopify: *Everything you need to start selling online—today*	Twitter: *Create and share ideas instantly, without barriers*	Zappos: *Deliver WOW through customer service*

Younger generations are your toughest consumers and they want to associate themselves with a cause. They want to be inspired to make a difference. So, does your association represent independent gas companies (yawn) or is it helping bring cheaper gas to the United States quicker (wow!)? Does your chamber of commerce connect businesses (yawn) or does it bring in an average of $25,000 in new business to members each year (wow!)? See the difference? When you talk about your association and what it does, it shouldn't sound like a textbook or instruction manual or a bill on Capitol Hill (yawn!). Make sure it's meaningful, unique, and motivates people to take action. Grab your audience, get them to sit up and say "wow!" and they will gladly join you.

A few additional tips to keep in mind when crafting your association's value proposition are:

Placement

According to the National Center for Biotechnology Information, 17 percent of website page views last less than four seconds. That means you don't have much time to get your value proposition across, so don't be shy!

You will see in the examples above, the value proposition gets right to the point in just a few words, and all of these propositions appear big and bold on the organization's home page.

One association I came across in my research dedicated an entire page to its Membership Value Proposition. However, the value proposition was difficult to find, took two clicks and scrolling to navigate to the page, and at more than 75 words it was entirely too long.

Gen Y is looking for a concise, easy to find message on what your association does and how the decision to engage in your association will bring value to their lives. You've got four seconds to capture their attention, so get to it.

Research

It's important that you ask members what your association does best, but take the extra step to compare your association's value proposition with your competition.

Knowing what your association does best requires some research of your association's competition and getting clear on how your association's membership is better. You don't have to be the best in every way. Associations have a tendency to want to tell people their life story when they should be only talking about what they did for breakfast. You don't have to be the best at everything and fearful of losing a member who might be interested in that one thing you do once a year. Stop trying to be everything to everyone and focus on being the best and most important to someone. If you're the best in at least one way you're the best option for the people who value that aspect. Apple doesn't have the largest product selection. Amazon isn't the most prestigious. Tiffany's isn't the cheapest. And that's okay because people buy from them for other reasons.

Something has to make you the best option for your target members. Otherwise, you don't have a good reason for anyone to join or engage, and that's the kiss of death.

Assurance

Abstract phrases don't work anymore. Not to mention the millions of dollars it takes to connect the abstract phrase with the product. "Just do it" may have been a catchy slogan but it doesn't identify how your association is better, nor does it make the decision-making process for your prospective members any easier.

Also, your association could promise the world, but it won't gain any traction until its specific about how membership makes a difference in members' lives. That's why a retailer's promise to "save you money" doesn't succeed as much as an offer to "save you $30 a month."

The Membership Value Proposition I mentioned above—the one that was difficult to find and too wordy—started off with something about being part of the largest and only association and being a voice for the industry. When I scrolled further down, I saw the proposition promised delivering $500,000 in ROI (return on investment)! This association has completely missed an opportunity here. *This* is the value proposition—and a great one at that!

Can you describe how membership in your association could be valuable to, or better yet, make a difference in Gen Y's life? If not, this should become your association's mission.

Many association leaders make the mistake of thinking that the simple act of launching a Facebook page will make them relevant to Generation Y. This is the equivalent of throwing a wrench at the *Titanic*.

It's time to realize, and accept, that social media or apps don't drive the changes we're observing; it's driven by a shift in values. Changing your association's value system to cater to one generation may seem like an impossible feat or absurd business practice, but Trickle-Up Economics proves otherwise.

CHAPTER 3

Holding on to Your Flight Risks

*"I don't understand why the associations I belong
to are always publishing articles and talking at
events about recruiting members. I'm here and I'm
a member. Why is the association overlooking that
and taking it for granted? I don't want to hear or see
the association complaining about the need for more
members. It's annoying! That's not my job; it's theirs."*

Young Professional
Chicago, Illinois
Age: 26

When Michael Nevergall attended college, he was ecstatic to receive a
tuition-reducing offer from an association. As long as he purchased a
membership in the association each year, the association, through an
alliance with the university, would reduce his tuition. Substantially. "I paid
$1,000 for membership and got $12,000 off my tuition. It was a great deal,"
Nevergall recalls. At 31, Nevergall is still a member of the association, but
he's both unhappy and unengaged.

Nevergall realizes the association's tactic was to lure in student
members, and credits the association for being smart and proactive in
their approach. However, beyond the tuition reimbursement, Nevergall
said the association has failed miserably at engaging young graduates.

One example of this generational oversight: The meetings come with a
high price tag and are all held during lunch in a busy section of a large city.
"It's presumptuous," Nevergall said. "The association just thinks everyone
will want to come to them. What they don't take into consideration is that
attending their events will cost me $50 for lunch—and that doesn't include
parking—or that I will have to commute and take three to four hours out
of my day just to get there. It's just not worth it to me."

Nevergall has hung on to his membership, evolving into an unengaged
"checkbook member." He realizes he could have easily dropped his
membership as soon as he graduated or anytime since then, but Nevergall

keeps thinking about that $12,000 in tuition and feels guilty. So he continues to pay his dues, feeling unhappy—even resentment—towards the association and refusing to engage.

Nevergall is considered a flight risk, disengaged and highly likely to drop his membership. His story is just one small example in a sea of change that's rapidly moving more young professionals into "flight risk" status.

Forget the recession. The biggest challenge companies will face in the next five years is yet to come: A mass exodus of employees from the workforce. Baby Boomers have already begun retiring en masse and scant few organizations have any kind of succession plan in place to recruit and groom future leaders.

It's not like they haven't tried. You can't open a *BusinessWeek, Fortune,* or *Forbes* magazine anymore without seeing some kind of list of the best places to work, best places to intern, or best places to launch a career. That's because corporate America has recognized that reaching the young and restless generation isn't as easy as it sounds. It requires new approaches to how people are managed, how the work gets done, and how fun, flexible, cool, and rewarding the whole experience is.

It's like we're trying to disguise work so it doesn't really look or feel like work anymore. As crazy as that sounds, it's what's driving the decisions from the top because, according to the 2013 *Cost of Millennial Retention Study* the harsh reality is that it's costing U.S. employers between $15,000 and $25,000 to replace each Gen Y employee they lose, and 60 percent of Ys spend less than three years per job. That's a very expensive revolving door.

No one is certain whether this revolving door is an age trend (every generation was more likely to switch jobs in their 20s), a generational trend (Gen Y leaves jobs faster and more often than other generations), or a social trend (more technology results in more restless behavior and the shifting job market results in more opportunities and allows for job hopping).

Regardless, turnover is happening and will continue to happen. As stated previously, we're on the brink of the largest shift in human capital in history with an average of 10,000 Boomers already retiring every day in the United States and continuing to do so for the next 15 years. Our businesses, nonprofits, and associations will desperately need Generation Y to engage, and all desperately need to prepare for this shift.

Keep in mind the following:

1. **Turnover presents an opportunity.** Members will likely look to your association to help them train or find young talent, succession plan, and sell businesses.

2. **Turnover will impact your association's leadership.** One association executive I spoke with told me she is observing a retirement wave in associations, seeing four of her peers announce retirements within a matter of a few months and several others preparing to retire within the year. Furthermore, the job sector of membership association as defined by the U.S. Bureau of Labor Statistics has a median employee age of 48.6. This is listed at number 14 among the oldest category out of 322. So whether you realize it or not, the association industry is aging.

3. **Turnover will impact membership.** Be prepared. As the Boomers commence the retirement process and younger generations move in, you may find that membership trends and engagement change. Membership might not naturally accompany an entire career, it may become something episodic, customized, or on-demand.

Perhaps Generation Y will never settle into a workplace and stay much longer than three years. Perhaps they will continue to be flight risks, but your association can and should prepare for any and all shifts in engagement. From a membership perspective, there are measures that can be taken to slow the revolving door and elongate the amount of time Ys engage, whether as employees, volunteers, or members.

Membership Engagement Redefined

First of all, we need to define membership engagement. Some association leaders make the mistake of thinking an engaged member is anyone who pays dues each year without question. Others believe an engaged member is one who sits on the board of directors. Still others will define engaged members as those who attend all the events or read all the e-newsletters.

In light of what we've learned thus far about Generation Y, I believe membership engagement is something else entirely. I think membership engagement is the emotional commitment the member has to both the association and the association's mission.

Membership engagement is not showing up for meetings or writing dues checks anymore. It's not just being in a relationship with the association. Engagement—or at least the expectation of engagement—is evolving into something that positively impacts self, the association, and community or industry all at the same time. Allow me to explain.

I previously worked for a metropolitan chamber of commerce with a board of directors of 50 people. Every single person on that board was a high-profile leader and the chamber loved to boast of its connections to the city's most influential leaders. But being a board member is not the equivalent of being engaged. This harsh reality came into focus when the chamber was experiencing one of the most tumultuous times in its history, losing substantial membership and revenue, experiencing considerable turnover within the staff, and the board invested little time or effort to remedy the situation.

It's not that the board didn't know how to help, it's that they didn't really care. No one wants to admit this is happening, but it's a common occurrence within associations. I consult with many associations each year and the lackluster support of the board is frequently apparent because the board is usually populated on outdated or self-serving criteria.

The chamber had a reputation for being a notable community organization and the chamber recruited a board to further that reputation. But peel away the self-interests and you quickly realize this gentlemen's agreement forged between the chamber and the board was merely a façade. The board didn't want to roll up their sleeves and volunteer their help because they weren't especially passionate about the chamber and its mission.

This just goes to prove that showing up—even in a leadership capacity—isn't the same as being engaged. And if there's one thing we've learned about Generation Y it's that they won't show up unless they believe their participation is worthwhile and capable of making a real and significant difference.

Generation Y's values and behaviors have been shaped from being raised in a technology-driven, highly accessible, collaborative, sharing environment where solutions that make life easier, happier, and better are almost always within reach, as are the opportunities to help improve the lives of others. This will further the definition of membership engagement beyond just showing up because Gen Y isn't content with just showing up. In order for Generation Y to truly engage, they will need to really care about and be inspired by their involvement *and* the association's work.

When members care they use discretionary effort. The engaged member willingly volunteers her time working on projects for the association. The engaged member promotes the association to his peers without being asked simply because he values his membership.

At 36 years old, Byron Patrick is the second youngest person to serve as board chair for the Maryland Association of CPAs. While Patrick is technically a young Gen Xer, he relates to the values of Generation Y and offers up his perspective as someone who got involved in an association immediately after college and has now moved into leadership.

In 1999, Patrick landed his first job at a CPA firm. His boss was chair of the Maryland Association of CPAs that year and shared with Patrick the association's need to re-energize and focus on a younger generation. Shortly thereafter, Patrick was asked to participate in the association's Under 35 Task Force. Their task was to recreate the association from scratch.

At the same time, an Over 35 Task Force was meeting and working on the same task. For nine months the two task forces worked independently of one another, then met to discuss and merge their ideas and came up with five bold steps to get the association where it needed to be.

Reflecting on the task force initiative, Patrick describes it as an "awesome" experience. "I worked with other CPAs, forged great relationships with them, and became intimate with the association. After that, the association became the core of my professional life." Upon the task force's conclusion, he jumped into committees and other task force initiatives, referring to himself as evolving into a "MACPA rat." In 2008, he was nominated to sit on the board.

Patrick's engagement cycle is not unlike the cycle of most Gen Ys whom I interviewed for this book. There seems to be a clearly defined path for engaging this generation:

- Step 1: Someone whom the individual admires invites you to attend or join the association;

- Step 2: The energy within the association is inviting, the leadership is open to innovation, and the association's value is immediately apparent and easy to understand;

- Step 3: The opportunity to do something influential and meaningful (gaining beneficial skills or contacts while helping the association, community, or industry) is immediately available;

- Step 4: The outcomes of your work are apparent and your contributions are appreciated;

- Step 5: You are invited to continue to be in a relationship with the association via new opportunities and steps 3–5 repeat.

"The energy in this association is really unique. Tom (Hood, CEO) is an infectious guy and the association and leadership emulates that positive attitude," Patrick explained. He adds that even as one of the youngest board chairs, frequently being among a "congregation of much older chairs," the association and its leaders are always forward-thinking and have never made him feel too young to carry the torch.

"These people have more passion for the industry than most and when I was put in a room with them it energized me. Then they opened up opportunities for me to help with strategic planning and leadership. I was giving my time and walking away with all this training and knowledge. It's been awesome. Once I got involved and drank the Kool-Aid, I couldn't put it down."

Note that Patrick is referring to his membership experience as a very powerful emotional connection, built upon the behaviors and values referenced in the first two chapters of this book. It's based on a meaningful and personal relationship, not on revenue.

Revenue or Relationships

Ask any association leader whether their focus is on revenue or relationships, and they will undoubtedly insist their focus is on relationships. Every association believes they excel at collaboration, networking, community, and fulfilling a big and meaningful mission. But let's get honest, people. There's a business side to what you do, too. And for decades, associations have measured success in terms of quantity: number of members, number of people attending events, number of chapters, even number of board members.

As a result, associations would do just about anything to increase their numbers. Think about member-get-a-member campaigns, dues promotions, bundled and early-bird pricing, and even tuition reimbursement as in Nevergall's case. Within associations there's always been a push for more: more meetings, more members, more attendees, more board members with deeper pockets and broader influence. It's all fueled by the desire for more revenue. Unfortunately, there hasn't been the same drive or focus on generating meaningful relationships and relevance. There are people who will read Nevergall's story and think the association succeeded. (So what if Nevergall isn't involved! That's his choice. At least the association is getting his dues payment, right?) Likewise, some would argue there will always be "checkbook members"—people who submit their dues checks but don't actively participate—and that's okay.

But I'm not convinced.

I think accepting dues payments sans member engagement as the norm is just another way of putting revenue above relationships. What would happen if the association that Nevergall continues to pay out of guilt actually contacted him and asked him why he hadn't showed up for a single event? Perhaps Nevergall could share his opinion, be empowered to help the association reach other young professionals, become an active member, and the association would gain his active participation eventually leading to more revenue. Furthermore, Nevergall may begin to appreciate his membership, feel good about it, speak positively of it, and actually promote it. Nevergall would establish an emotional connection with the association, much like Patrick did with Maryland Association of CPAs.

A successful association will recognize that ownership behaviors—paying for a membership you never use—are dwindling. A successful association will realize there is considerable upswing to putting relationships first, and not revenue. A successful association will understand that quantity isn't the same as quality, and Generation Y could care less about quantity. Ys are obsessed with quality and return on investment.

After all, Generation Y has been referred to as the Trophy Generation, a term coined by Ron Alsop, author of *The Trophy Kids Grow Up* (2008), because they have always been rewarded for participation and not achievement. This changes how they expect to be treated and what they want in return for their time and money.

Trophy Kids

Generation Y is the most protected, supervised, provided-for generation in history. At a young age, they were shuttled off to playdates and soccer practices, leading very structured lives in comparison to any other generation. Parenting and teaching styles changed substantially, and Gen Ys were lavishly praised and often received trophies when they excelled (and sometimes when they didn't) to avoid damaging their self-esteem. In fact, according to Alsop, this generation was treated so delicately that many schoolteachers stopped grading papers and tests in harsh-looking red ink.

Their Baby Boomer parents aspired for the corner office and title of president and CEO, and they raised their children to do the same, placing a high premium on success including academic accolades, philanthropy, sports, and other extracurricular activities.

Not surprising, a generation raised receiving trophies just for showing up expects a significant return on investment from their employers, membership associations, and any place they spend their time. These trophies come in the form of feedback, attention, guidance, and opportunity—all which are relationship-based. It's difficult to foster an emotional commitment to your association and its mission when any of the following hurdles stand in the way.

Distrust

During the past 40 years, trust in each other and many institutions has been dropping steadily. These years were marked by events that furthered distrust—like junk bonds, Monica Lewinsky, Enron, Catholic church sex scandals, September 11, and the Iraq war. Generation Y has come of age during the worst recession in 70 years, graduated with insurmountable amounts of debt, and they've been raised in a media-saturated world observing in great detail the nation's leaders lie and fail to deliver on their promises. As a result, Gen Ys don't readily trust. You have to earn their trust. So be transparent and avoid keeping all your board's meetings and decisions private. And if you commit to doing something, do it. No excuses.

Hierarchy

Generation Y employees want to feel like a part of the community from day one, not something they have to work hard at achieving by "paying their dues" figuratively or literally. Associations are notorious for fostering a good ol' boys club culture based on who you know and what you've achieved. If you're holding your young members back from sitting on the board or participating in a project simply because they haven't been in the workforce for more than 20 years then you are, in essence, telling them that they are just a number, simply paying dues and taking up a seat at the annual meeting. Remember, this generation was told by their parents that they can do anything they set their mind to. Holding them back from that potential in your association will confuse, frustrate, and alienate Generation Y.

Offline

Anyone under the age of 32 has never known a world without technology. And yet, so many associations still slog by on websites that haven't been updated since 2008, rarely update their Twitter feeds—if they have one—avoid apps, and still fear Facebook. There's only one thing that can be said in terms of technology. If you aren't using updated technology, you aren't speaking the same language as Generation Y. Consider yourself irrelevant.

Minimal ROI

In the past, it was enough to provide insurance discounts and membership directories. That era is long gone. This generation has access to more information, contacts, products, services, and education than any other generation. They've always been rewarded for participation and not achievement. They are the most entrepreneurial generation in history, and also the most supervised and provided-for generation. Needless to say, this generation is going to expect great things in return for their time and resources, depending on an emotional commitment to both the association and the association's mission.

California Dental Association (CDA) has taken a strategic approach to furthering the association's emotional connection with members. In 2012, the association created a new role on staff: Member Concierge. Terry Fong, a CDA staff member for 26 years, now spends her days calling on all of CDA's new members—as many as 1,000 per year—to welcome them to the association and ask "Is there anything we can do for you?"

A typical week for Fong starts with a printout of the previous week's new members, followed by placing a phone call to each one. She speaks with about 60 percent of the members she calls. During the call, she gathers some key information, such as employment status, key interests, reason for joining, and languages spoken. All of this then goes into CDA's member database. Fong also shares highlights from her conversations with CDA staff.

By the end of the week, Fong follows up with an email to each member she spoke with and typically includes attachments or links to resources pertinent to their discussion. The call and email kick off a planned sequence of welcome messages via email and postal mail throughout the member's first year. Fong sends a check-in email to each new member at six months and one year, as well.

Some early signs show a positive impact from Fong's work. A year after she started, new member retention outpaced the previous year's numbers and enrollment in CDA's professional liability insurance among new dental-school graduates increased by 17 percent.

While the focus on revenue may have worked for associations during the past several decades, it doesn't work anymore. Generation Y won't be content just to have a transactional relationship with your association for the sake of simply being affiliated and part of your community; the return on investment has to be greater and it starts with a meaningful relationship.

Campus Life

Even fraternities and sororities are re-focusing on relationships. It would seem that fraternities and sororities—associations comprised entirely of Generation Y—would have all the answers when it comes to engaging this generation. You might be surprised to know that's not always the case, but there is still much to learn from the associations focused entirely on engaging Generation Y.

"The value proposition has changed for my generation. When I was in a sorority, we had to stop assuming everyone wanted just to be a cool kid. That's not the case anymore. My generation wants real benefits, academic help, and community service projects," recalls Ashley Sullivan, COO, New York State Trial Lawyers Association.

Mark Koepsell, CAE, would agree that Greek life isn't about being a cool kid, but it is about having a cool factor. Koepsell has been working in higher education for 17 years and is currently the CEO at Synergos, an association management company overseeing the Association of Fraternity/Sorority Advisors and the Association of Fraternal Leadership & Values.

He says the arrival of Generation Y has changed fraternities and sororities drastically, marking clear differences between this generation and the generations that have come before. "Traditional thinking doesn't work. This generation views tradition as old school and it really turns them off," he said.

After some trial and error, Koepsell's associations seem to have discovered a recipe that works with engaging Y members based on these concepts:

- **Inclusion**

  Generation Y has to feel included and valuable to the association. This means being open to new ideas and staying informed on—and using—the latest and greatest trends or technology. Most of Koepsell's staff has degrees in college student affairs. This was intentional because Koepsell wanted to hire people who knew the college student environment well and could easily relate to their student members.

- **Experimentation**

  As Koepsell puts it: "We've built experimentation right into our culture. That means it's good to try new ideas and it's okay to fail." In fact, Koepsell always sends someone from his staff to the South by Southwest Interactive conference to observe the trends.

- **Cool Factor**

  Synergos doesn't just use social media to communicate with their association members. Rather, Koepsell said they go the extra mile to make their members feel like celebrities on Twitter and elsewhere.

Events feel like a rock conference with an absolute cool factor. "We go for polish. I call it the icing-on-the-cake moments," Koepsell said.

Josh Orendi, owner of Phired Up, a consulting company specializing in fraternities and sororities, explains that recruiting has been a priority for fraternities and sororities since the post-World War II era. Problems started to arise when today's Greek organizations relied on the traditions and processes of the past.

During the past few decades, Greek life had become more focused on producing bigger and better events. This process spiraled out of control as frats and sororities simply tried to out-do one another. In the process, Greek organizations started to become more insular to the point of being detrimental.

Orendi explains that when Greek organizations shifted their focus off of building relationships, stigmas emerged, Greeks started socializing only with other Greeks, the organizations stopped growing, and membership declined because nothing about this process was valuable to Generation Y. "People don't join frats, they join people," Orendi noted. To engage Generation Y, Greek organizations must return to their roots as friendship clubs and focus on building authentic, credible relationships, "getting back to conversations, not events."

Chris Beaman, assistant director of membership and chapter services for Kappa Delta Pi (KDP), an international education honor society, said KDP is investing in relationships to curb membership decline. At 25, Beaman has an advantage viewpoint. "In order to appeal to and retain my generation, the association has to be supportive," he explained. "It's realizing members own the relationship with the association and that's a shift. It used to be the association owned the relationship with its members."

KDP is serving its chapter leaders in a variety of ways in hopes of helping them do their jobs effectively and also to boost the recruitment and retention of members. For example, KDP provides guidebooks for each chapter leadership position, posts best practices and ways for chapter leaders to collaborate on the organization's website, oversees a healthy chapters initiative, and Beaman travels to each region for face-to-face meetings once a semester.

Also, KDP empowers its chapters to introduce changes. "We dare our chapters to change and to ask, 'What are we doing on autopilot and really need to change to better serve our members?'" Beaman said.

As Koepsell explained, the most difficult part about engaging Generation Y is that you can't just push "repeat." Associations always have to be evolving and that's both challenging and opportunistic.

At KDP, every Friday the staff engages in team conversations, setting aside two hours to collaborate and discuss pressing membership issues or to explore hot topics. When it comes to Generation Y, the innovation never stops. Associations have always experienced turnover, but the arrival of Generation Y brings new and heightened expectations to the forefront. Associations that struggle to adapt will be at risk for increased flight risks. While this forces an association to really consider and communicate the benefits of engaging, let's not overlook the fact that it's also forcing associations to be their best.

Associations won't be able to rest on their laurels and bask in their brands anymore. Generation Y will expect associations to be influential, powerful, meaningful, and inspirational. Generation Y will only engage in the associations that make a difference in their lives and the lives of others. And I think that's a good thing.

CHAPTER 4

Culture Shock

*"Sometimes I feel like I don't belong because of how
hard it is to get involved in the governance structure in
some associations. I feel like popularity and favoritism
are present sometimes and it's hard to break through
to become more engaged when you are new to the
association and haven't had a chance to build your
network of peers. Nobody knows your name? Then
you might just be a nobody. Sad, but often true."*

**Young Professional
Washington, DC
Age: 30**

In 1996, two students at Stanford University conducted a research project that would eventually grow into a business earning $50 billion in revenues and attracting one million job applicants each year.

From its inception, Google became renowned for having a workplace culture that was truly revolutionary. This has attracted many Generation Y employees. In fact, Google's average employee age is 29.

Success has certainly followed. Google has continually earned honors as the best company to work for in the United States, Canada, Japan, India, Korea, Brazil, and others. The free cafes, funky offices, and games are among Google's trademarks, but according to a Think Quarterly article authored in 2011 by Laszlo Bock, Senior Vice President of People Operations, the perks that generate all the press aren't the reason for Google's success. Rather, Bock credits three cornerstones of Google's culture for its differentiation and success: mission, transparency, and voice.

Mission

Google's mission is to organize the world's information and make it universally accessible and useful. That's nice rhetoric, but Google goes the extra mile to make the mission something real and tangible. This creates an arena where data and people are literally brought together in surprising ways and employees are engaged in the process. This acute focus on mission has a huge effect on who decides to join Google, how much engagement and creativity they bring to the company, and even on how they feel and behave.

Transparency

Google leadership shares everything. The company hosts a weekly all-hands meeting called TGIF, hosted by Google's leaders. In the first 30 minutes, the team reviews news and product launches from the past week, demos upcoming products, and celebrates wins. The second half of the meeting is dedicated to Q&A. Everything is up for question and debate, from the trivial to the ethical.

Every quarter, Google's executive chairman presents to all Googlers virtually the exact materials that were presented to the board of directors at their last meeting. Google's intranet includes product roadmaps, launch plans, and employee snippets (weekly status reports), alongside quarterly employee and team goals so that everyone can see what everyone else is working on.

By giving employees more context about what is happening, how, and why, the additional information enables employees to do their jobs more effectively and contribute in ways a top-down manager couldn't anticipate.

Voice

Believing in a greater good and knowing what's going on are important, but people then need to be able to translate their beliefs and knowledge into action. Google has many channels for expression, recognizing that different people—and different ideas—will percolate up in different ways. The channels include but are not limited to direct emails to any of the leaders, various sites and listservs, Google+ conversations, and a wide range of surveys.

Google regularly surveys employees about their managers, and then use that information to publicly recognize the best managers and enlist them as teachers and role models for the next year. The worst managers receive intense coaching and support, which helps 75 percent of them get better within a quarter.

The largest survey, "Googlegeist," solicits feedback on hundreds of issues and then enlists volunteer employee teams across the entire company to solve the biggest problems. This fosters a robust, data-driven discussion that brings the best ideas to light, so that when a decision is made it leaves the dissenters with enough context to understand and respect the rationale for the decision, even if they disagree with the outcome.

The bulk of what Google does to cultivate this creative, passionate workforce costs nothing, yet it's yielded substantial returns. Founded by two Gen Xers and heavily supported by a Generation Y workforce, Google was built on the premise that people want meaningful work, knowledge of what's happening in their environment, and the opportunity to shape that environment.

Other companies make similar products, yet employees are drawn to Google because working there means something more than just working for an internet service and product company. In fact, Google is successful for reasons that have very little to do with what the company actually does.

Some association leaders make decisions based on nothing other than membership trend reports, surveys that ask members what time of day they prefer to attend events and whether they read the monthly magazine, and historical perceptions of how the association should be performing.

All of this is creating incomplete, flawed assumptions about what's driving membership. Then, when membership declines, the first inclinations are to lower dues, slash conference prices, invest in elaborate marketing campaigns, host a top-secret emergency board session, or distribute a survey. These are all attempts to try to get members to behave the way the association wants them to behave (join, renew, engage), but they tend to be short-sighted and ineffective. Why are they ineffective? Because there are only two ways to influence a person's behavior: manipulation and inspiration.

Take a look at all the great organizations out there, and you'll find one thing in common: They don't sell things. They stand for things. When you sell, you put yourself in the position of having to convince people you are worth following and this always requires manipulation of some kind, be that manipulating price, product, positioning, or marketing message. Manipulation is a trick, and tricks only work for so long before people grow tired of them.

Conversely, when you stand for something, you inspire. You take a stand for something, usually bigger than yourself, and people relate. It motivates rather than manipulates. Inspiration has the potential to magnetize individuals, communities, and nations. Inspiration is relevant across all age demographics and never goes out of style. It's always trending.

Associations have the power and opportunity to inspire. Unfortunately, I've seen several suffer from analysis paralysis, negativity, and dues debates, all while neglecting their most valuable resource in the process: the membership experience.

A friend of mine tells the story of a time she was working on a huge consulting project for an auto repair and maintenance franchise. Her task was to identify ways to increase the franchise's profitability. She spent a great deal of time visiting the company's locations and interviewing employees and customers. A few months later when she sat down with the company's executives and they asked her anxiously, "What is your recommendation? How will we increase sales?," she asked them, "It's simple. Improve your waiting rooms."

The executives were shocked and disappointed with her advice. Certainly waiting rooms weren't the answer! They were more interested in hearing about revolutionary and elaborate marketing strategies, business models, and areas for improving productivity. My friend assured them she had included all those items in her plan, but that if the company didn't invest in their waiting rooms first, none of it would matter.

"The customer experience is crappy—your waiting rooms are dark and dirty and the receptionists aren't especially friendly," she told them. "And if the customer doesn't feel good upon walking into your place of business, the customer won't want to return. Then it won't matter how many radio ads you produce or how productive your business is running. The customer experience has to be exceptional. Improve your customer experience and the money will follow."

Association leaders take note: Improve your membership experience and the membership will follow. I've had the opportunity to interact with associations worldwide and I've interacted with few associations that can boast of great cultures. As with auto repair, I can tell you with absolute certainty that culture makes a significant difference in how effective an association is at recruiting and retaining members and generating revenue.

Culture is not something you can actually see, yet it is in the environment and experiences your association creates for its members. Think of culture like a smell or song. The smell of a freshly baked cake or a song from childhood can evoke certain memories and feelings, and it's those feelings—whether good or bad—that are very powerful influences.

Your association's culture is exactly the same. The association could be doing amazing projects or providing unique services, but if members don't feel good about their membership experience, they won't engage. Culture can't be singled down to one thing. It's evident in all the association's behaviors, habits, and every interaction with your members. It's how members feel when they talk to your receptionist on the phone, visit your association's website, attend an event, and meet your board of directors.

Culture has always been important, but right now it's crucial. Culture matters to Generation Y more than to any other generation.

This generation has been given the negative label of being entitled, and well—they are. Their expectations are set a little higher and their patience is a little shorter because they have been raised in a world driven by technology and credit cards. This is the instant gratification generation accustomed to having the world at their fingertips (literally). They have been given more choices and access than any other generation, so they've never had to settle for inadequate, irrelevant, or unhappy and they're certainly not about to start.

The only way your association will stand a chance at engaging Generation Y is if the association's culture is positive, engaging, and service-oriented, thereby making the membership experience exceptional. Cultures that are non-inclusive, close-minded, stagnant, or unfriendly will repel rather than attract this generation.

Is Your Association Toxic to Generation Y?

Not sure if your association's culture is toxic to Generation Y? Here's a quick quiz to help you find out. Simply answer true or false to the following statements:

___ The association is more driven by executive or board-level direction than by membership needs.

___ Leaders (board and/or staff) are showing signs of frustration, fear, or negativity frequently or more often than usual.

___ Staff are leaving the association or thinking about it.

___ The association is experiencing declines in recruiting members.

___ The association is observing declines in membership retention.

___ Absenteeism is increasing—members not showing up for meetings or events.

___ Members are expressing negative feedback or showing apathy towards the association.

___ Leaders have a tendency to blame others and make excuses for their mistakes rather than accept ownership and take responsibility.

___ Staff or committee leaders can't make any decisions without receiving specific approval from the executive team or board prior to doing simple tasks or taking care of members.

___ Gossip and behind-the-back conversations are common throughout the association.

___ 10 or 12 hour days are not uncommon for the staff.

If you answered "false" to all of the statements, congrats! But if you answered "true" to at least one statement this is putting your association's future at risk.

Make no mistake about it—culture is almost entirely influenced by the association's leadership. In all of the research and interviews I did to prepare for this book, it became apparent that even with a core of engaged and passionate members in place, their efforts won't get very far very fast without the support of the association's leadership. And the minute that leadership squelches Gen Y's enthusiasm they're headed straight for the door.

Really good leaders recognize the influence they wield and won't pass blame when membership takes a nosedive. I've heard every excuse in the book from leaders who blame younger generations for their membership woes:

- "They haven't grown into membership yet. When they get older they will join."
- "They simply aren't joiners. They don't value membership like we did."
- "They're getting married and having kids."
- "They're busy with their careers."
- "They don't have jobs."
- "They're too busy."
- "They're entitled."
- "They're broke."
- "They're lazy."

Here's a radical thought: What if associations spent less time dismissing Generation Y for having character flaws or being immature, and more time focused on creating the best association experience possible for them? Would this change in approach yield different results?

Absolutely.

No one wants to be ignored or made to feel insignificant, more problematic, or less deserving than anyone else. This is especially true with a generation dubbed the Trophy Generation, known in the consumer world for their unwavering focus on quality and great service, and renowned for their YOLO (You Only Live Once) attitudes.

Culture matters to a generation driven almost entirely by personal happiness. They will refuse to engage in anything negative, stressful, unorganized, or draining of their time and energy. Generation Y expects a great experience and wants to affiliate themselves with a great cause.

So what can associations do to improve their culture and remain relevant to the YOLO generation? Here are some suggestions:

Inspire Excellence

I saw someone get fired over a misspelled name once. An association I worked for hosted a large event with hundreds of people in attendance. The association president noticed the last name of one of the board members was misspelled on his nametag. Immediately upon returning to the office that day, she pulled the event director into her office and fired her.

The president later made a speech to a shocked staff. She reminded everyone that we were in the service business and that when we failed to serve our members to our utmost abilities and to continually strive for excellence, the brand would falter, the membership would lose faith and trust in us, and the entire association would suffer.

In the following weeks and months, everyone on staff was deathly afraid of making a mistake, yet that incident ultimately shifted our focus in a positive direction. When challenges popped up, we found ourselves asking is this the best we can do for our members?

Membership culture has really transformed. In previous decades, joining an association was more about carrying on a tradition and service to community and industry. Generation Y doesn't have the same instincts. Yes, the aforementioned are important, but this generation is motivated when they truly love their membership experience *and* the association's mission.

The pursuit of happiness is a very real need Generation Y wants to fulfill. Despite this generation's ample opportunities and choices, this generation has also been raised in an era of school shootings, economic decline, terrorism, and debt. Research shows they aren't the happiest generation, which is probably why they've made happiness their quest in every facet of work and life.

Whether you agree or disagree with the association president's decision to fire someone over a misspelled name is not really the point. The point is that you need to ask yourself whether your team exemplifies the association's purpose or brand of putting members first. Like it or not, this example brings to light two culture-related transitions:

1. Your association will reap what it sows.

The people who interact with your members have to fully appreciate and understand your association is in the service business and that the culture they create for your members plays a critical role in your association's ability to succeed.

This is an awesome responsibility not to be taken lightly, especially considering Generation Y is drawn to people and experiences and not organizations.

The fact is, you don't easily make people who are good, great or people who are great, excellent. The most successful organizations will always start with excellent—the talent and stakeholders that get it will create a place members want to be.

2. All the world's a stage.

Shakespeare coined that phrase centuries ago, and it's quite relevant in today's social media-saturated world. Associations will have to bring their A game each and every time because whatever is the best is spread immediately, as is the worst. The market picks a winner instantly now, through reviews which are based on experiences and organizational culture. Mediocre and satisfactory simply aren't good enough anymore. There's excellence and there's everything else.

Focus

Sooner or later everyone experiences something like this: you buy a red car, thinking a red car is unique, and suddenly you are seeing red cars everywhere. Why does this happen? Because you are focusing on red cars and you get more of what you focus on. Laura Goodrich shares the theory of focus in her book, *Seeing Red Cars* (2011).

Think about it. Have you ever sat in a board or staff meeting and someone is saying: We *don't* want membership to continue to decline, or We *can't* afford to do that, or We *won't* be able to change? What is the focus in these situations?

According to Goodrich, consciously and unconsciously we tend to focus on what we don't want, and because that's what we're focusing on, that's what we get. In other words, if your association is focusing on membership decline, you'll probably just get more membership decline. Coupled with a side order of more negativity, frustration, and despair.

It's the underlying force of fear that gets in the way of solving problems and shifts our focus onto what we don't want rather than what we do want. To stop fixating on the fear of change, association leaders must rewire their brains to focus on positive outcomes. In order to do that, the association's stakeholders must get really clear on what they want to achieve. If change begins with focusing on what you want, then focus on what you want to change. Start by writing down your responses to these questions:

- What won'ts, don'ts, and can'ts are holding me back?
- What won'ts, don'ts, and can'ts are holding the association back?

Next, write down what you want for yourself and for the association. Declare your intentions in a way that it is exciting, specific, measurable, and timely. (Example: Rather than "I want to read more," consider "I want to embrace reading a book a week that helps me grow and expand personally and professionally.")

- What do I want to achieve?
- What do I want the association to achieve?

Change begins with you and your focus.

Take the Cornerstone Credit Union League for example. The league is composed of 700 member credit unions throughout Arkansas, Oklahoma, and Texas. In 2007, the league studied its participation among Generation Y and realized the number of Ys visiting credit unions was significantly small.

"Credit unions were employing them but they weren't part of our meeting and they were certainly not on our board. If you looked at our board it was all gray hair," recalls Rick Grady, vice president of research.

Cornerstone appointed a task force composed of members of the board and Gen Y staff. The task force met for nine months. In the end, the task force realized there were several changes the league could make to engage Generation Y. Cornerstone made immediate and significant changes including:

- Adding Gen Y representatives to the board of directors;
- Hosting meetings around the state, specific to getting Gen Ys together;
- Launching a Facebook page, Twitter account, and mobile app;
- Hosting a Young Professionals Conference focused on helping young professionals with skill development and career pathing;
- Offering opportunities for young professionals to meet with representatives of Congress;
- Launching an advisory committee comprised entirely of young professionals to provide recommendations and feedback to the league; and

- Asking young professionals to play a key role in developing the league's annual conference.

"We're moving young professionals into the mainstream of the association and the mainstream of our member companies," Grady said. "I knew if we didn't make a change, at some point the Boomers will retire and the majority of the credit union business will go away." Grady said credit unions really missed the Generation X market because they didn't pay attention to it. "I didn't want us to miss an opportunity with Gen Y, too. Some members of the older generation were so reluctant to change. That was tough, but we just had to come to the realization that some people may get left behind."

Success has followed. Grady said the league has observed increased attendance and participation across the entire league. CEOs of member companies are taking a stronger interest in mentoring and succession planning, as well. "I've seen a mental change in our league. Generations are working together and when Boomers speak to the younger generation it's constructive and not dictoral. Plus, more Gen Ys are moving in and want to be involved." It is possible for change to become something that is not feared, but desired.

Start at the Top

In my work with associations I've come to realize that there's usually an influencer, or core group of influencers, within an association that drives the agenda and sets the tone. You may be surprised to learn this person isn't always the executive director, CEO, or board chair, and it isn't always a positive influence. I've observed all types of influencers in action, from especially negative and outspoken board members, to executive assistants undermining the association CEO, to the disgruntled member who leaves and starts a competing association.

As I mentioned previously, Generation Y is the most protected and supervised generation in history. From bike helmets to car seats and never eating in a cafeteria that serves peanut butter, they've been carefully tended to since they were infants. They also experienced very structured, busy childhoods and were shuttled to playdates, soccer practice, and numerous activities from the time they were toddlers. In fact, their parents have been dubbed Helicopter Parents for constantly hovering over their children and being continually present in their lives.

What does this have to do with membership? Well, quite a lot actually.

Helicopter Parenting forged a unique relationship between parents and their Gen Y children, which has influenced this generation's views of leaders and relationships in the workplace.

Previous generations spent a great deal of time without adult supervision, leaving home on their bikes in the morning and instructed by parents to be home by dark for dinner. Naturally, these generations became independent and self-sufficient at a young age. In fact, it was an expected and anticipated rite of passage to move out of your parents' house soon after graduation.

Then Generation Y comes along and the child-rearing pendulum shifts from independence, freedom, and using your imagination to one of structure and scheduled activities focused on almost constant learning and achievement. Parents started giving up their free time to focus almost entirely on their children's lives and activities.

In addition, children were treated as little adults and given an equal voice in the household. In fact, this generation is the first to influence the majority of household purchasing decisions. In 1997, when Gen Y was between the ages of 2 and 15, the article "Getting Inside Kids' Heads" in *American Demographics* reported children 12 and younger were influencing $165 billion in purchases ranging from food to household items, computers, and vacations.

The 1995 "Kiddie Cars" article in *Brandweek* reported that children influenced $9 billion worth of car sales in 1994. A car dealer was quoted in the article as follows: "Sometimes, the child literally is our customer. I have watched the child pick out the car."

Creating an exceptional membership experience for Generation Y begins with exceptional leadership. Not the hierarchical kind of leadership, but the "I want to know you better and create something really inspirational together" kind of leadership.

Here are three shifts in leadership to take under advisement:

1. Generation Y doesn't understand hierarchy.

This isn't a generation whose parents told them to "be seen but not heard." They've always been asked to share their opinions on just about everything. Not only that, but their parents actually acted on their opinions—repeatedly. As a result, this generation often struggles with working in a hierarchical environment or being part of an association where leadership and opportunity is reserved only for those with the most years of experience.

2. Generation Y wants to be inspired.

Generation Y has been raised in an era of technology, where it's possible to be in touch with anyone, anywhere, anytime. They have never known a time when the boss reigned supreme and had all the answers. That's the stuff of myths and legends to this generation because the internet has always provided them instant answers and instant access to experts on any subject. The way they look at leaders is different than other generations and ever more situational. Their most important criteria are following a leader who will walk the talk and derive their authority from having a genuine, inspiring sense of purpose.

3. Generation Y wants a relationship.

This generation spent childhood and adolescence in close proximity to their parents and that usually resulted in having a close relationship with their parents. They expect to have great relationships with the people they work with, including an opportunity to have access and relationship-building opportunities with their leaders. Generation Y tends to look up to and be loyal to the leaders that foster a relationship with them and exemplify their values in innovation, transparency, and making a difference.

The leader of a culture-driven association will be thought of more as a person devoted to a cause than as an executive running an association. When others try to describe him or her, they will think of the vision first. The culture-driven leader constantly demonstrates passion and energy for the work to be done and is surrounded by people who do the same.

Byron Patrick, board chair of Maryland Association of CPAs, described executive director, Tom Hood, as an "infectious guy" and the entire association and leadership emulates his passion for the association. As a result, the staff has "more passion for the industry than most people." It was this passion that persuaded Patrick to get involved in the association.

Ashley Sullivan, COO of New York State Trial Lawyers Association, credits the association's executive director for the association's high energy environment. "My boss is excellent at hiring. He doesn't see gender, age, or experience. He's more concerned with whether you have the "it" factor. If I have the motivation to try something new, he let's me take the initiative to do it."

The associations that survive the 21st century will have leaders in place who are knowledgeable about industry and employee trends, open to innovation and collaboration, and capable of lighting the spark that motivates others—especially Generation Y—and moves the association toward the future.

Ask the Tough Questions

I'm not a big fan of membership surveys, largely because I think 99 percent of the surveys out there are entirely too long and don't ask the right questions. If you really want to get to the heart of the membership experience, you can't be asking questions about newsletter frequency and social media use.

You need to ask members what's inspiring, what's frustrating, and how membership has made a difference in their lives. You need to think like a Gen Y and be authentic, transparent, and efficient about your communication efforts.

For example, 15Five is an employee feedback platform designed to effectively and simply improve employee engagement and internal communication. It's based on the simple idea of having each employee spend 15 minutes a week writing a report that takes the manager no more than 5 minutes to read. By responding to a question each week like, "On a scale of 0 to 10, how happy were you at work this week" and "What aspect of our company do you worry about the most," a company can get much-needed and incredibly honest feedback from its employees, thereby identifying any problems that exist within the culture and remedying them.

I'm not suggesting that associations survey their membership each week, but I am suggesting associations must find ways to get vulnerable and brutally honest with their members. Having the courage to be vulnerable and accept your shortcomings isn't something that comes naturally in the business world or associations. For centuries organizations have been buttoned up, cautious, and set on portraying a positive image with a successful track record. That's really done nothing but lead organizations to spinning the truth, fabricating false identities, communicating in ineffective corporate-speak, and has even led to the untimely and unfortunate demise of many organizations. Generation Y is wise to these tactics and won't tolerate them. Really knowing your membership, what inspires them, and what irks them is the best way to further your relationships and create a culture that's truly meaningful and engaging to them.

Know Y

Just as it's important to know—really know—your membership, it's essential you really understand the generation your association is trying to reach. Reading this book is a good first step, but don't stop there. Don't just take what I've written here as sufficient information. Do your own research. You will be a better association because of it.

Engage in as many conversations as possible with people who fall into the Generation Y age category. (As of 2014, these are people who are between the ages of 19 and 32.) To be more specific, I would encourage you to have 30 conversations in 30 days with people in this age category. That may seem quite overwhelming, but these conversations don't have to be lengthy. They can be done via phone or Skype, and will yield unparalleled insight to your target market.

At minimum, ask each person these two questions:

1. Consider a situation when you really felt like you belonged. Specifically what happened that made you feel like you belonged?

2. If you could create the ideal membership experience—one that provides you with value, meets your expectations, and makes a difference in your life—what would you create?

Jot down notes from each conversation, identify any repeated answers or key themes, and share your findings with your colleagues in the association. This exercise is most effective when a group (i.e., membership committee, board of directors, association staff, etc.) works on this during the same month, then reports on their findings.

Don't know 30 Gen Ys? Start with who you do know then after each conversation, ask for references to other contacts in this age category. This is one of the best and most effective ways to do market research, and in the process you will forge new relationships and visibility for your association.

It's surprising to me how many associations make assumptions or try to guess what younger generations want without actually engaging in conversations with them. Remember: Your goal is to create a membership experience that is relevant and engaging to Generation Y, so actually knowing Generation Y is essential.

Future-Focused Association

Considering how much change is happening, it makes sense that a really strong association culture will be adaptable to change and primarily focused on the future. "There's no beige here," says Rachel Whitman, events and development manager at Nexstar Network. Indeed, the association's offices are brightly colored, yet another way that Nexstar Network defies tradition.

Founded in 1992, Nexstar represents nearly 500 independent home services contractors in plumbing, heating, air conditioning, and electrical trades. The association provides comprehensive support for their member companies offering 65 training classes per year, three regional conferences, and one national conference. But that's just the tip of the iceberg.

Nexstar also assigns each member a business coach and a marketing coach, and provides access to customized advertising and a strategic partner program featuring 150 partners. Members receive quarterly rebates for using these services that they can apply towards their dues.

Nexstar's online bulletin board is private to members only. No strategic partners are allowed access to the bulletin board, which generates as many as 100 posts per day. The association helps members of the Nexstar board schedule meetings with members in their region. The association provides scholarships and provides trades training to military personnel through their Troops to Trades program.

Whitman says Nexstar is different than other associations because "we do what our members want, not what we want." Nexstar refers to this as M1 which stands for Members First. Several of Nexstar's members are family-owned businesses. Whitman said in many cases, it's the next generation business owner—the Gen Y—taking an interest in joining Nexstar because it is so service-oriented and packed with real benefits.

Dues run higher than most associations with an initial fee of $15,000. Whitman explains the high dues attract the member that Nexstar wants. "We want to attract those businesses that want to grow; the ones that are working on their business—not just in it. Growing a business means making a time and money commitment and that's where Nexstar can help."

Not only does Nexstar boast a positive member culture, but its employee culture is equally beneficial. Whitman described Nexstar as a "bootstrap organization" not a 9-to-5 organization. "We all get really connected to our members. At Nexstar if you have a meeting scheduled and a member needs something, you cancel that meeting without question. Our members trump everything. If you don't really care about your members you don't have an association. Membership is everything."

Associations were built on the premise of community and belonging, yet in recent years many have lost sight of that purpose, because well, the times they are a changing. But culture is what we need to hold fast to, not only because it really matters to Gen Y and is central to engaging them, but because it matters to everyone. After all, without culture

Google would just be another technology company. Without culture, your association is just another group of people paying dues to have meetings together. Without culture, there's no value, no competitive advantage, and certainly no reason to show up.

CHAPTER 5

Pollinators and Digital Natives

"My generation has a different social structure than previous generations. Regardless of an organization's purpose, I believe social interaction is one reason why members stay involved. Advances in methods of communication no longer require people to meet in a group at a pre-specified time to socialize and interact."

Alexander Keppler
Age: 26

Here's something to ponder: Is your association home to a grassroots intelligence network or a playpen? Is your association thinking about creating something that's a generation better or is it a generation behind?

In his book, *The Steve Jobs Way: iLeadership for a New Generation* (2011), author Jay Elliot, former senior vice president of Apple and a close colleague of Steve Jobs, wrote about Jobs' approach within Apple.

Elliot explained that under Jobs' leadership, Apple fostered an entrepreneurial environment, always challenging and encouraging employees to share their ideas and creativity in alignment with Apple's vision. He wrote:

Through encouraging employees and their ideas, you get a grassroots intelligence network. Employees bring in new things in the market and talk about them, discuss their advantages and shortcoming, test them, play with them, and then wonder, What can we do that's a generation better?

In contrast to Apple's approach, Elliot writes that in traditional companies, people are so focused on productivity and profits that they don't have time to look at things from a radically different perspective. As a result, there isn't much cross-pollination, because too many companies keep a playpen for really bright people, separating them from the rest of the organization. This limits the potential of the employees and the entire organization. So which category does your association fall into—one that fosters grassroots intelligence or one that monitors intelligence via a playpen?

I've seen evidence of playpens in several areas of associations, which tend to separate board and staff and members into their own categories and sometimes the two never meet. I worked for an association that didn't allow the staff to interact with the board. Only the association president was allowed to meet with board members. I've since learned this isn't all that uncommon. I've been a consultant to many associations where board and staff are mostly estranged.

I've also seen associations create young professionals groups simply to appease a young group of members who want to be more influential in the association. The association doesn't want to give them any actual influence yet, so they create a playpen where younger members can congregate and have their own board of directors.

I've also come across association staff who complain their member companies won't invite the participation of younger employees because company executives are concerned about poaching and another company might meet and steal their young talent. So the association creates a playpen for the senior executives and a playpen for younger employees, not allowing any crossover of either age group into either playpen.

Not surprising, these are also the associations grappling with membership turnover, negative cultures, and a lack of innovation. Regimentation isn't beneficial, in fact it's quite detrimental to an association because it inhibits the cross-fertilization that creates innovation, and its era has long since come to an end. In the post-war era, when the Baby Boomers came of age, companies took a lesson from the military and applied systems to absolutely everything for increased efficiency, predictability, and productivity. It worked, then. But now we've moved out of the Industrial Era into the Knowledge Economy, which is powered by innovation and requires organizations to adapt to an interconnected, globalized economy where knowledge and expertise are as critical as other economic resources.

This isn't new information. The Knowledge Economy was first identified in the 1990s, yet here we are nearly 20 years later, and associations are still struggling to transition from having playpens to creating grassroots intelligence networks.

Generation Y has come of age during the Knowledge Economy; they have little to no memory of the Industrial Era and therefore no appreciation or understanding of processes and traditions and doing things the way they've always been done.

This is a generation that has only known a world powered by the trademarks of a Knowledge Economy: innovation, interconnectedness, globalization, and expertise. Anything else will seem foreign and irrelevant to them. They will struggle to comprehend why the bylaws can't be changed, why decisions can't be made on the fly, why they have to join a chapter to be part of an international association, and who the heck Robert is and why associations are still using his Rules of Order.

Associations rooted in the past are really going to struggle to engage a generation progressing towards the future. Generation Y's habits, perceptions, and behaviors are radically different for a reason. These are the Digital Natives and Pollinators, after all.

Digital Natives

Generation Y is the first generation to have never known life without technology. We all know this to be true, but do we really comprehend what that means? It means this generation prefers never to be more than literally a few feet away from a technology device. Nielson reports that 83 percent of Ys actually sleep with their smartphones and they are twice as likely (40 percent) to use social media in the bathroom. It means this generation values access to technology more than dating among other things. It means this generation considers access to technology a basic need, valuing it as much as freedom and oxygen on basic needs assessments.

Crazy as it may sound, Generation Y can't fathom a life without technology because they've never known life without it. I hope this helps to put into perspective how important technology is to your association's future. Simply put, if your association isn't using technology in every aspect of the way it does business and interacts with members, it is alienating this generation and completely irrelevant to them.

The Digital Natives, a term coined by writer Marc Prensky to describe Generation Y, is the generation born into the digital technology era. They are emerging as the world's dominant demographic, while the generations that came of age during the analogue age—the Digital Immigrants—are getting smaller.

As Digital Natives, Generation Y is more reliant on technology, more comfortable using technology, and tends to be among the first to try new technologies in comparison to the generations of Digital Immigrants. The typical Gen Y owns multiple tech devices including smartphones, tablets, and gaming systems, and constantly multitasks across these platforms.

Yes, every generation is using technology to build relationships and buy products and services. (There's that Trickle-Up Effect again.) These elements are present in all generations, it's just that Generation Y has maximized the use of the tools with which to express themselves on a much broader scale. It is this extreme dedication to and comfort using technology, combined with ongoing advances in technology, that have empowered this generation in new and different ways.

Generation Y is often criticized for not being capable of effective interpersonal communication, but that's largely a myth. It's simply that the approach has changed. Gen Y has been raised in collaborative environments, shuttled off to play dates and soccer practices since they were toddlers. Beginning in early adolescence, Gen Y's social outings consisted mostly of hanging out in groups, be it shopping, dining, or traveling. They enjoy hanging out in coffee shops and being in close connectivity with other people.

Of course, technology has furthered their communication and relationship-building strategies. As social creatures, who have been networked and encouraged to collaborate their entire lives, Generation Y loves being part of the global conversation that social media affords. As much as the Baby Boomers and other Digital Immigrants might want to ignore the glut of "tweets" and "likes" on the cloud, and dislike that Ys are actively sharing their selfies and opinions, social media cannot be underestimated in its far-reaching capabilities.

The Millennial Consumer, a report published by Boston Consulting Group in 2012, explains that Generation Y is more likely to use the internet "as a platform to broadcast their thoughts and experiences and to contribute user-generated content." This is why the Digital Natives are far more engaged in activities such as rating products and services and uploading videos, images, and blog entries than the Digital Immigrants.

The rapid pace of users sharing and distributing information with each other makes it all the more important for associations to engage members in meaningful interactions that make them truly empowered participants, whether it's sharing photos, asking questions, or posting interesting news.

At full disclosure, I'm not a social media expert and you really need an expert to work on your association's social strategy. But if you find yourself woefully behind and needing to jumpstart your social media presence on a shoestring budget, here's a quick and easy four-step process for getting social on the right track.

Step 1: Set a goal

Set a realistic goal for your association. For example, maybe you want to add six new student members each month. Maybe your members are companies and you want to add three new companies each month. When you use a realistic number as your goal, you can track the increase or decrease in sales at the end of the month.

Step 2: Help Your Customer

Once you set your goal, determine how you're going to use social media to help you achieve it. This does not mean you are going to focus on marketing messages and sales tactics. Shift your association's focus off of "what can we sell you?" to "how can we help you?" Social media is fueled by great content that isn't salesy and that people will want to share, so determine who your target customer is for your goal, what their needs and challenges are, and different ways your association can help them.

Step 3: Merge Into Traffic

Your messaging will fall on deaf ears unless you post it where the traffic is already headed. Where does your association generate the most traffic? Via Facebook, LinkedIn, Twitter, or something else? If you aren't sure which social media networks drive the most traffic to your site, use this opportunity to analyze your web traffic using Google Analytics.

After you execute your social media strategy for 60 days or so, compare the results and you'll know which social networks drive your website traffic and where you should focus your efforts.

Step 4: Build Your Content Strategy

"When it comes to technology if you don't have a plan then you have a very big problem," said Ashley Sullivan, COO, New York State Trial Lawyers Association (NYSTLA). She said NYSTLA is live streaming classes for CLEs, going digital with their materials, focusing on SEO, and highlighting a member benefit each month via social media. When the NYSTLA Young Lawyers Committee hosted a rooftop event, the association captured video and created a follow-up video montage, set to music, and posted it on YouTube "so the members who weren't there could see what they missed."

It's good to find out where your traffic comes from so you can spend more time where your target audience spends theirs, and then generate helpful content that's useful to your audience. For example, Jimmy Fallon gets the most traffic via YouTube and Twitter, so he posts show previews on YouTube and Twitter and tweets during live events. Make a list of helpful posts you will create, and then share the posts with your community manager. Use a content calendar to let everyone see what's publishing on which social media networks and when. As you develop content, remember to include a call to action. Give your online followers a place to go or something to do. Whatever your ideal end result is, use calls to action that will help your audience get there.

It goes without saying that technology is a defining member benefit for Generation Y. If your association isn't using technology in every aspect of the way it does business and interacts with members, it is alienating this generation.

Social media is so big to this generation because they can self-select how and when they get it. That's huge insight into what makes this generation tick. Because of technology, Generation Y will be more averse to slow paces and long-term approaches to change. Because of technology, they value customization, convenience, consumer reviews, and globalization. Because of technology, they will want to learn, lead, and engage with your association in unique and different ways. This is not to say Generation Y doesn't want face-to-face experiences. It is to say that technology is their go-to resource and falls into their comfort zone. For some associations, technology has opened the door to increased engagement.

The Bar Association of San Francisco (BASF)

The Bar Association of San Francisco (BASF) spent a lot of time examining how Generation Y learns. After numerous interviews and thorough research with Gen Y members, BASF recognized this generation wanted a plug-and-play at your convenience learning model. However, when the idea to introduce online CLEs was first introduced, it was met with dissension.

According to Yolanda Jackson, deputy executive director and diversity director, there was widespread fear in the association that by placing the CLE option online, the association would lose business and lose an opportunity to connect with members face-to-face.

As difficult as it was to take that leap of faith it's made a huge difference for the association. The revenue from online CLEs has more than doubled for the association—with representatives of every generation using the online option—and the number of in-person CLEs has continued to grow every year since the online option became available.

Jaycees

For 90 years the Jaycees had been organizing community development projects and developing next generation civic and business leaders, ages 18 to 40. Once renowned as a unique organization fulfilling a unique need, the Jaycees started to lose hundreds of members when it faced considerable competition from other organizations, technology-based networks, and economic decline. The association is in a recovery phase, regaining traction among Generation Y.

The association started by taking a leap of faith and going all digital and will soon be all video. Joel Harper, executive director, explained the association first eliminated printed materials, like the quarterly magazine. Then they eliminated e-newsletters. Now, Jaycees produces a five-minute video newsletter twice a month called JCTV. Each episode is professionally produced, lasts less than five minutes, and the on-air personality gives viewers (Jaycees members) the information they previously would have read in print. Most of the Jaycees trainings are done in webinar format and recorded, so members can watch them at a time of their convenience. Jaycees shares email addresses of the trainers so members can interact with them directly and ask questions.

"Many of our e-documents in our web library, like position descriptions and bylaws, will soon have a video counterpart that gives the viewer an overview of the document, pointing the viewer to read the document to find out more," Harper added. "This is a generation of people with short attention spans and so far our attempts at being more technology-focused and more hands-on have been well received by the younger generation."

Professional Convention Management Association (PCMA)

Another example comes from the Professional Convention Management Association (PCMA), which hosted its first hybrid conference in 2011. Approximately 3,700 people attended the live conference in Las Vegas, and over 500 participated digitally in interactive sessions. The response prompted PCMA to begin delivering a wide variety of digital programs on a regular basis. By the end of 2011, it had an active and engaged community of 2,000 registered digital users. Then, when the 2012 conference rolled around, PCMA realized a 9 percent increase in event registration. Of the nearly 3,800 live event attendees, 14 percent said their digital experience played a significant role in their decision to attend in person.

In an article following the conference, PCMA's CEO, Deb Sexton, was quoted as saying that PCMA was fortunate to have a leadership team that believed in taking risks to move the association forward. Just to be clear, Sexton is conveying the process of integrating technology from the association's side, describing the move to digital as a risk is a perspective common among Digital Immigrants. But when it comes to Generation Y, they will never think of access to technology as a risk or a luxury. In fact, just saying that using more technology is risky or difficult is likely to turn Gen Y off. To the Digital Natives, technology is expected. It's a necessity.

To be fair, the Digital Immigrants have been in for a tumultuous ride. At no other time in history has technology moved so fast. The explosion of technology in just the past 10 years marks the start of a new technology-dependent world. Hand-held devices, Bluetooth headsets, smart watches, and Google Glass are literally making computers an extension of body and mind, creating a Cyborg-like effect. The meteoric rise of social media outlets including Facebook, Twitter, YouTube, and Skype indicates that innovation will only press forward faster and faster.

We're rapidly moving toward becoming a networked planet, a sign that even developing nations will soon have access to technology, thereby closing the digital divide. (Presently, even those who don't yet have the technology still know that it exists.)

Connecting with one another in the modern world requires a knack for social networking and texting, which is the norm for the Digital Native. But for the Digital Immigrant, it can be akin to learning a whole new language.

Associations by and large have been slow to wade into the sea of technology change, frightened by the concepts of change and transparency. This creates an ever-widening gap between the Digital Natives and the association behaving like a Digital Immigrant trying desperately to forge a connection with them. Young people live in the context and traditional organizations see the changing context and struggle.

For the Digital Natives, the idea of a standard, IT-issued computer will seem as odd as a company uniform. Fifty-three percent of Gen Ys surveyed by Forrester already use multiple devices for work, and this is a wake-up call for associations that need to be as mobile-friendly as possible. From equipping conferences with stations for plugging in and powering up devices, to having a website that can easily be viewed on a computer, tablet, or smartphone, to investing in apps and using Twitter—technology has to be central to every association offering.

Of course, keeping up with technology will continue to be a challenge. Technology is moving ever faster. Consider Vine, Twitter's video service that enables users to create six-second looping videos, and Snapchat a photo messaging app that allows users to take photos or record videos and send them to a controlled list of recipients only viewable for 1 to 10 seconds after which they will be hidden from the recipient's device and deleted from Snapchat's servers.

Associations must find the courage to face the future—and fast—or they will most certainly get left behind. Here's a great example.

Doximity

Founded in 1847, the American Medical Association is the largest professional medical organization in the United States, representing over 224,000 physicians and medical students, according to the latest data.

Along comes Doximity, a social platform for doctors founded in 2011 that now has more than 707,000 member profiles. It is considered the largest, fastest-growing network for U.S. healthcare professionals, reaching 40 percent of all doctors in the United States. Here's why one in three doctors recommend using Doximity:

- Free to licensed physicians and medical students;
- Majority of platform decisions come from Doximity's member groups;
- Create a profile and share private contact information with select colleagues;
- Physician profiles are searchable and viewable to the public at users' discretion;
- Access to free eFax service for sending secure faxes between offices and pharmacies;
- Earn an honoraria for sharing your expertise;
- Receive updates on compensation trends in your specialty and geography;
- Gain access to latest medical news and numerous journal articles— earn Category 1 Continuing Medical Education credits as you read.

Doximity allows doctors to ask a critical mass of their peers any number of questions ranging from drug interactions to specialist advice. Needless to say, Doximity's arrival has generated a considerable amount of publicity and even controversy. Doximity's success has been credited to getting doctors the answers they want faster and more reliably than even a Google search can provide.

As this book has touted throughout, associations are challenged to meet the needs of members faster and better than ever before. Doximity took it a step further by creating a sharing platform, allowing doctors to be collaborative and engage in dialogue with their peers via technology. Such a move is especially relevant to Generation Y, the first generation to be raised with technology. Younger generations want access to information and are drawn to convenience and connections with people, not institutions.

Doximity's founder, Jeffrey Tangney, is 40 years old and has worked in 10 roles at six companies ranging from business development at a biotech start-up to healthcare investment banker and executive vice president of sales and marketing. Tangney, although not a Gen Y himself, is an excellent representative of a Pollinator.

Pollinators

At the beginning of this chapter, I mentioned the book on Steve Jobs' career, and that Apple allows for cross-pollination, which leads to grassroots intelligence networks. Traditional organizations still think in terms of silos and job descriptions and will likely despise the idea of giving up the command-control way of doing business—but now we have a generation coming into power that thrives on the concept of pollination.

Pollination and cross-pollination are terms used to describe a process that allows all people within the organization to contribute, share, and grow, while collaboratively extracting the golden honey (ideas or innovation) for the betterment of the entire organization.

Pollination is the outcome of the Sharing Economy (mentioned in Chapter 2) and the Knowledge Economy (mentioned in Chapter 4) fusing together.

To expand upon the pollination concept as a metaphor even further, Generation Y's lifestyle mirrors that of actual pollinators: bees. They tend to job-hop (buzzing from flower to flower), actively seek to quickly acquire information and skills (gather nectar), and willingly share their opinions and ideas via social media (pollinate).

Pollination thrives in a technology-driven world, but it doesn't survive on technology alone. Associations can use and benefit from the pollination process elsewhere.

"What do you do?" used to be a simple question. Individuals defined themselves by profession: teacher, engineer, pilot, or by company: IBM, NASA, Kodak, but it was always one job, one identity. Today's young professionals, however, aren't as easily categorized. They struggle to prioritize which job title to place on their LinkedIn profiles. They tend to work several jobs simultaneously, consult, and start up businesses while working for another company. This tendency towards multi-careerism—

referred to as the Gig Economy or "sidepreneurism"—is taking over the workforce.

Yes, economic factors undeniably fueled some of this multi-careerism, but even before the recession this generation was redefining and repurposing the concept of work. Prior to Generation Y, there was an order in life: finish your education, get a job, get married, buy a house. This generation doesn't do things in any one order. They do what feels right, feel less pressure to succeed using the traditional career path, and choose jobs where they feel they can make a difference. The unifying result is pollination.

This generation does not identify with one company or career. They don't work for IBM, but instead build smart computers. It might be a slight difference in semantics, but it underlines that their priorities are on their own skill set, and not on their employer.

"I don't know any Gen Y who self-identifies using only one 'job,'" writes *Forbes* contributor and a Gen Y, Larissa Faw. She has authored several articles on Gen Y and describes her generation as "hustlers" in her 2012 article, "How Millennials Are Redefining Their Careers as Hustlers." Indeed, Gen Ys aren't position players. They don't just play first base or left field. They are athletes, wired to do many things at once. This is key information for associations, which will struggle to sell Gen Y on taking on a three-year board position or hiring them to spend every hour of every working day writing articles for the association's magazine.

On the other hand, there's great opportunity for associations that recognize a large percentage of Gen Ys work several jobs simultaneously or start up businesses. They may be time poor, but make no mistake about it—they do make time for projects and people they see as beneficial to their careers and also invested in making a difference for their communities or industries. Associations certainly have something to offer.

Multi-careerism introduces multiple challenges and opportunities to companies that are trying to follow Google's example and allow employees to work on projects outside of work or trying to foster environments focused on pollination and the sharing of ideas á la Apple. Associations can certainly respond to this need by providing resources and training on the topic.

Multi-careerism and pollination are concepts that are ridding the world of silos, titles, and roles, which mean the walls between for-profit and nonprofit are also melting away and the two are becoming reliant on each other and in many ways inseparable. Here's how one company is capitalizing on this transition.

Engine for Good

Jim Delaney recognized the opportunity to add more value to the YMCA while sitting on the board of directors. "I wanted to do more than go to board meetings to provide advice and raise a little bit of money," he recalled. "I wanted to use my skills and experience to really dig into the challenges I heard the YMCA was having with capacity building. They also had great opportunities they just didn't have time to take advantage of. I saw an opportunity to make a greater impact."

Jim Delaney noted many nonprofit volunteer opportunities consist of one-day opportunities, helping out here and there with events and fundraising. Meanwhile, Delaney recognized that most of his fellow young professionals sitting on boards of directors were too busy with day-to-day demands to help the YMCA tackle big-picture challenges.

Delaney's idea was to put together small teams of rising stars at big companies, to tackle big-picture projects. He pitched it to the YMCA and recruited 24 volunteers to work on six projects. One team created a guide for social media use. Another created a 140-page best practices handbook after analyzing the best practices at each of the local YMCA's 14 branches and camps. The typical project would last about six months, after which the volunteers were free to move on or get involved in a different way. One of the volunteers is now on the executive committee of the YMCA board of directors.

In 2010, Delaney launched Engine for Good. Today, the company is building customized leadership and team-building programs for organizations, focused on teaming young professionals with community projects and professional development. It's a win-win-win for all involved:

- Corporations engage their rising stars in high-impact professional development and team-building opportunities, increase employee engagement and retention, and contribute to community;

- Nonprofits benefit greatly by getting on-the-ground help and advice from a group of highly talented, next generation professionals; and

- Young professionals receive personal and professional development, developing new skills and perspectives that will benefit them as they build their careers, as well as a more satisfying volunteer experience.

Associations tend to breed homogeneous cultures. The problem is, when you put people who think similarly together, innovation continues to diminish. In order to accelerate new thinking and stay relevant, associations must put people from different perspectives together. This will yield new ideas and better results. After all, your association might be considering line extension when it really should be doing a channel overhaul.

In addition, if your association is used to having the same people volunteer and lead year in, year out, pretty soon those fans get so immersed in your association, they see the association only through that lens. They neglect to see the association through the lens of someone younger, new, or different. It's difficult to solve a problem when you're not even sure what the problem is because you can't identify it or relate to it.

When I work on projects with associations, I will often recommend they speak to people who aren't members of the association. This idea is usually greeted with shock or fear, and that's part of the traditional culture Steve Jobs' tried to avoid. How smart, innovative, or responsive can you be when you are only talking to those you always talk to?

A 360-degree view of your association is extremely advantageous. Moving from outside to inside to outside and back again creates a boisterous dynamic. The fact is, no matter how big or successful your association is, there are always more ideas outside than inside. When you're thinking like a pollinator, you're looking far afield for ideas that you can translate and adapt for use in your association. Here are two pollination examples at work:

- In her book *Regional Advantage* (1996), Annalee Saxenian, dean of the School of Information at the University of California at Berkeley, explores the factors that contribute to the high levels of innovation and entrepreneurship in Silicon Valley. Essentially, Silicon Valley's innovation is robust because of the extensive cross-pollination of ideas between individuals and companies. Firms are concentrated in a small area, which leads to more informal interactions and easier formal connections. There are also essentially no barriers to communication between people of different backgrounds and socioeconomic levels.

- Twitter knows how important cross-pollination is to creativity. The company makes an effort to hire people with unusual skills, knowing that diversity of thinking will certainly influence the development of their products. A random sampling of people at the company would reveal former rock stars, a Rubik's Cube champion, a world-class cyclist, and a professional juggler. The hiring practices at Twitter guarantee that all employees are bright and skilled at their jobs, but are also interested in other unrelated pursuits. This results in random conversations between employees in the elevator, at lunch, and in the hallways that can lead to fascinating new ideas.

Think about it. If everyone guiding your association reads all the same trade magazines, attends all the same industry conferences, shares the same industry backgrounds and experiences, and talks among themselves about the same variations on a theme, you will continue to get the exact same results and engage the exact same people.

Beth Yoke, executive director of Young Adult Library Services Association (YALSA), said Generation Y tends to view associations as "circles of people" and not in a top-down approach. They dislike a rigid structure. "Our members really don't like our traditional volunteer structure, which is to apply via paper application, wait to hear back, then meet face-to-face with the committee for the required 12 meetings a year," she said.

While YALSA hasn't been able to change everything at once—they are a subsidiary of the American Library Association—they are making adaptations. For example, YALSA created a "Get Involved Infographic" to show ways members can get involved in the association without serving on a committee. YALSA also developed an iPhone app, introduced digital badges, and an advocacy infographic with a detailed companion text document to help members visually understand the importance of advocacy and how to get involved.

Associations are uniquely positioned at the intersection of industry and workforce development, talent development, and community development. Associations have an advantage. The ecosystem for breeding innovation and greater good is already in place. By using technology and pollination, associations can propel themselves into the future and do even more for the benefit of more people.

According to Jobs, "Success can be self-defeating if it leads you into the rut of repeating yourself. Too often we cannot envision a different world because we've gotten into the habit of looking at our world with the mind-set of what has worked before."

If you're looking to expand your membership pool to include a Gen Y cohort, your first step is getting into the hearts and minds (and digital footprints) of Generation Y. Here are a few examples of associations that have done just that.

e-Books

The National Science Teachers Association (NSTA) is creating iPad-ready e-books to help teachers become more comfortable with content that they may not have extensive training in. Videos, simulations, and interactive elements make the content more engaging for educators. Assessments and activities allow teachers to check their own understanding of the material and can be used with students in the classroom.

Gaming

American Institute of CPAs launched an interactive, online accounting game, Bank On It™, featuring more than 1,000 questions inspired by content in accounting textbooks. The game challenges students on accounting fundamentals and real-world workplace scenarios in the context of an online board game. Designed by high school students, Bank On IT™ weaves in real-life professional scenarios, reinforces principles taught in the classroom, and is mobile-friendly so students can play from their smartphones.

Digital Badges

The Center for the Future of Museums (CFM), an initiative of the American Alliance of Museums, introduced a form of online education in which members receive a publicly visible "badge," or number of badges, for completing assignments. Each badge level opens with a video, followed by additional information, then a written assignment which the participants can complete at their own pace. The site is password-protected and participants are encouraged to share thoughts in discussion forums.

Apps

Young Adult Library Services Association (YALSA) uses a Teen Book Finder app. Funded by the Dollar General Literacy Foundation, the app has a simple interface that allows users to access the full catalog of YALSA's book awards and selection lists. The app features daily "Hot Picks" and users can search by title, author, genre, year, award, and booklist or build a personalized list of favorite titles.

CHAPTER 6

Experience Generation

> *"My father is 53 and he's been involved in associations*
> *in the past. He's asked me, 'Why not you? Why not*
> *join an association?' He doesn't quite understand*
> *that there's little benefit for me at the moment.*
> *I haven't had the most stand-out experience with an*
> *association in the past where I'd want to immediately*
> *join, so I don't feel compelled to do so right now.*
>
> **Young Professional**
> **Assistant Project Manager**
> **Age: 27**

In 1953, Walt Disney wrote a proposal to potential financial backers for something that would be a new experience in entertainment. The proposal began as follows:

> The idea of Disneyland is a simple one. It will be a place for people to find happiness and knowledge. It will be a place for parents and children to share pleasant times in one another's company: a place for teachers and pupils to discover greater ways of understanding and education. Here the older generation can recapture the nostalgia of days gone by, and the younger generation can savor the challenge of the future.

"A place for people to find happiness and knowledge" conjured such a wonderful image that Disney quickly found financial backers. Today, Walt Disney World is known as The Happiest Place on Earth. However, most parents don't take their children to Walt Disney World only for the venue itself but rather to remember the experience for days, months, even years afterward. Thus far this book has addressed the Sharing Economy, Gig Economy, and Knowledge Economy, and there is yet another economy to add to the list: the Experience Economy. This economy is based on the premise that future economic growth lies in the value of experiences; goods and services are no longer enough to differentiate and compete amidst technology, increasing competition, and heightened expectations of consumers.

All these emerging economies simply point to the volume of change that's occurring in every aspect of how we live, work, and do business—and further support the fact that the generation that's come of age in this era of change is considerably different than the generations that came before.

Walt Disney World offers an experience, as do Apple Stores, Cirque du Soleil, the Geek Squad, Dave and Buster's, American Girl, TED Conferences, and Chuck E. Cheese. Some economists believe experiences have emerged as the most valuable commodity.

According to the book *The Experience Economy* (2011), authors B. Joseph Pine and James Gilmore explain advances in technology and increased competition have forced businesses into an ongoing search for differentiation. The book explains that in the 1950s, the Service Economy overtook the Industrial Economy, with services employing more than 50 percent of the U.S. population. By 2009, manufacturing and farming had severely declined, and services comprised nearly 90 percent of the jobs. (Globally, 42 percent of jobs are in service, 36 percent in farming, 22 percent in manufacturing.)

As the Service Economy grew and more competitors popped up, the consumers' desire for increasing and better service grew, as did the lack of differentiation between service providers. This introduced constant price pressures. So automakers, for example, increased the coverage and length of their warranties while financing and leasing cars. Associations have certainly fallen prey to the Service Economy's downfall. How often does your association discuss the price of dues and the need to offer bigger, better benefits?

I know of several associations worried about preserving their hold on the market as continuing education credits and other benefits have become available for free or significantly lower costs via other providers on the internet. I'm also familiar with many associations concerned about the growing number of competitors and the inability to provide something different. This makes achieving "must-have membership" status and growth nearly impossible.

Throw in big box retailers like Walmart, the bundling and "productization" of services (such as including tax preparer software in the purchase of a computer), offshoring work to India or moving manufacturing to China, and other attempts to cut costs and compete strictly on price, and one can draw the inevitable conclusion that goods and services are no longer enough to compete.

Experiences have emerged as an opportunity to create value and a competitive advantage in an oversaturated market. Buyers of experiences value being engaged by what the company reveals over the duration of time. Experiences are more memorable and considered more valuable than goods and services.

Experiences can offer enjoyment, knowledge, diversion, beauty, change, and access. Experiences affect who we are, what we can accomplish, and where we are going. Cornell psychology professors discovered that buying experiences actually make people happier and give them a greater sense of well-being. Similarly, economic research indicates happiness now comes from doing over having, not unlike the Sharing Economy concept explained in Chapter 2.

All this is great news for associations, which have the advantage of being in constant communication and interaction with their members. In the Experience Economy, associations have an opportunity to thrive—as long as the association can deliver a great experience to Generation Y. Let's take a closer look at the pillars of interaction among associations, members, and prospects and determine how marketing, causes, and events can provide the most memorable experiences with Generation Y.

Marketing for Generation Y

The decision to pay attention to, read, or share your content is more than coincidence—especially when it comes to Generation Y. This generation is often dismissed as being overly engrossed in their smartphones and wasting precious time on social media.

In May 2013, *Time* magazine's cover featured a 20-something taking a selfie under the title, "The ME ME ME Generation." Second paragraph in, the article referred to Generation Y's "narcissistic personality disorder." Well, we've already covered that topic in great detail here. Generation Y does have a higher sense of self because they are the most supervised, protected, provided-for generation in history. Like it or not, for better or worse, the fact is the world has literally revolved around this generation since they were infants. But while everyone is busy pointing fingers and slapping labels on Generation Y, there are some other facts that remain vastly overlooked and help to explain changes in values and behavior.

AMC's show *Mad Men* is about the wildly creative, alcoholic, and chauvinistic advertising industry in the 1960s. In the pilot episode ad man Don Draper is confronted with the challenge of building an advertising strategy for a cigarette company. At the time, the tobacco industry faced growing evidence from medical studies that their product was actually dangerous and deadly. So ads claiming "More doctors smoke Camels than any other cigarette" were no longer acceptable.

Draper is faced with the impossible task of repositioning cigarettes. His solution, in a moment of inspiration, is to change the message to focus on a small part of the drying and curing process involved in making cigarettes; toasting the tobacco leaves. His two word tagline is: "It's Toasted." The client shares that all their competitor's cigarettes are toasted as well—to which Draper replies, "No, yours are toasted. Theirs are poisonous." That's the power of positioning.

Yes, we still see brands focus on positioning. Like Coors, which focuses on being frost-brewed and even created cans on which blue-colored mountains appear when your beer is "Rocky Mountain Cold" and optimum for drinking. Logic would tell us the blue-colored mountains appear when the beer is put into any refrigerator, but positioning tells us this beer can is unique, intuitive, and therefore the beer is colder and better tasting than any other beer out there.

But Don Drapers of the world hang on to your three-martini lunches because positioning is now taking a backseat to emotion. More than that, the process of positioning, marketing, and advertising doesn't exist in a vacuum anymore. Companies don't have power or control over their messages—the power and the messaging is shifting to the consumers themselves! In fact, whether your association realizes it yet or not, your association isn't marketing its brand; Generation Y is. The conversation has shifted. Your association doesn't control the message anymore.

Purchases still don't have a whole heck of a lot to do with logic. It's still an emotional transaction, and heavily reliant on positive experiences. But if you still think Generation Y are narcissists obsessed with tweeting, texting, and selfies, you are wrong. There's actual neuroscience, social theories, and evolution biology behind Generation Y's social decision making.

The Social Media Effect

Research has uncovered the science behind social media. The better your association understands the motivations behind the behavior, the more likely your association can succeed at engaging this generation. Let's start with a story about Joe.

Joe is a 27-year-old professional. Joe wakes up one morning, walks out the front door and takes a selfie with the three feet of snow that have piled up on his Toyota Prius. He tweets out the photo with the header "OMG, that is A LOT of snow!" He gets a few comments and retweets from friends.

An hour later, Joe arrives at work, logs into Facebook and finds a friend's link to a prank website for a "Push Up Muscle Shirt" that is part of an Old Spice viral ad campaign. Joe likes and shares it.

Later that day, Joe logs into LinkedIn, spots *Fast Company*'s latest post on social media and sends it off to the other guys in his marketing department. They were just talking over social media strategies the other day, so Joe thinks the article could help the entire group.

Here's the skinny: When Joe and millions of other Americans wake up and tweet about the weather, Instagram their breakfast, or send a Snapchat, they're getting one undeniable benefit: brain candy.

In 2010, researchers at Rutgers University discovered 80 percent of social media posts were announcements about people's immediate experiences. Status updates like "OMG that is A LOT of snow" or "Eating yummy pancakes" are the norm in social feeds.

In 2012, two researchers at Harvard University expanded upon this research to see how self-disclosure affects the brain. It turns out that talking about our own thoughts and experiences activates the rewards system of the brain, providing that same shot of dopamine we get from sex, food, and exercise. The reward activity in the brain is also much greater when people get to share their thoughts with others. Simply put, Joe's tweet gave his brain pleasure. The Old Spice share on Facebook was even more beneficial.

Research shows that sharing a picture, video, advertisement, or really any content achieves more than a chemical reward—it is an act of self-creation. People are most likely to share an advertisement of the brand they associate with their self-concept and see as entertaining. Joe likes associating himself with the manliness represented in the Old Spice Man and he's entertained by the ad itself. As a guy who uses deodorant (maybe Old Spice), Joe is involved in the product category. Once again, Joe gets dopamine for sharing this and he's also boosted his self-concept.

Then Joe chooses to share a helpful article with his co-workers. In dozens of studies, researchers have found that the acts of cooperation and altruism, just like the act of self-disclosure, activate the dopamine reward system. In fact, the experience of being trusted is inherently rewarding. Instead of keeping the article to himself and passing off the insights as his own, Joe used the opportunity to help his co-workers. His brain rewards him for this act of cooperation.

What does all this science mean for associations? It means associations need to focus on creating great experiences, content, and opportunities that ultimately help people feel good about themselves and feel especially smart, important, and happy.

Joe and other Ys won't pay any attention to your association's content unless it's aligned with their values and aspirations. Associations have to think less about marketing their own messages and think more about what they're doing and saying that improves the quality of Joe's life (and the lives of other young professionals like Joe).

Your association has a unique opportunity to assist Joe in the creation of his social identity and the achievement of his own goals—which include the real pleasure of sharing information that will help and entertain friends, family, and co-workers. Give Joe tools to get dopamine, look good, and pay it forward in his community or industry.

STARBUCKS

One renowned company embracing both the principles of the Experience Economy and the values of Generation Y is Starbucks. With more than 20,000 stores in 61 countries, Starbucks has become the largest coffeehouse company in the world. Generation Y has driven much of Starbucks' success. Buy coffee at a fast food place and it will cost between 79 cents and $1.50, whereas coffee at Starbucks would cost $2.50 to $5.00. That's because Starbucks creates an experience for its customers and its brand is synonymous with quality.

Here's how Starbucks draws in the youngest of coffee drinkers:

- **Digital**
  Starbucks heavily interacts via social media. The Starbucks Instagram account has more than two million followers. Campaigns like Tweet-a-Coffee (which allows you to send a $5 Starbucks eGift Card via Twitter), and the Starbucks app allow Gen Y to connect with each other through social media, share their interests, and create even more sales for the company.

- **Rewards**
  More than 70 percent of Ys have said they will always come back to a brand they love. (Still think Gen Y isn't loyal?) Starbucks successfully takes advantage of this loyalty by offering benefits like free music and app downloads for participating in the rewards program.

- **Space**
  Even though Starbucks is a highly digitized company, it still evokes the feeling that it is part of the community. From family-style seating to high-top tables, the coffeehouses are designed to provide an environment that encourages face-to-face interactions.

That's how marketing has changed for Generation Y—it's fueled by science and emotion and it's grassroots. Plus, this shift is certainly having a "Trickle-Up Effect" when you see how social media use among all generations has increased in recent years.

And Joe's selfie may seem narcissistic, but I assure you that Toyota loves that Joe posted that selfie and promoted the car's brand! When Generation Y loves a brand or an experience, they see it as an extension of themselves, and part of their identity. The same will happen to your association. If Joe receives great information or opportunities from his association experience, he will advocate on the association's behalf. At minimum, he will become a brand ambassador for your association. At best, he will engage in the association as a member.

When first-year medical students at the University of Alberta created a video parody—complete with choreography and unique lyrics to a few Disney tunes—the video went viral and attracted media, generating considerable publicity for the university. In interviews, the students explained that they made the video on their own time, using their own singing and dancing talents. This is the very definition of brand ambassadors!

If your association is going to build trust, loyalty, and advocacy with the Joes of the world, it must do so outside the bounds of the traditional advertising relationship. Don't use social media to try to sell membership. Instead, help people achieve personal satisfaction through your association—through experiences—and the sales will come.

Strategies

Associations really miss some golden opportunities when it comes to marketing because they aren't being authentic or because they jumped on the social bandwagon before really thinking it through. Whether pitching an idea or trying to convince someone to buy something, everyone wants to know what content will engage the audience and get them to sit up and take notice. But we don't often ask, what is the experience of someone who consumes the information?

Remember: We're all drawn to experiences, which is why Disney World is such a popular experience. Furthermore, Generation Y has been raised in the Experience Economy, which explains why this generation's decisions to engage are heavily influenced by experiences and emotions.

So think like Disney and go the extra mile to make your audience feel smart, important, and happy. Here are some tips on how to create the experiences they want through your marketing efforts.

Stories

One of the best marketing strategies is simply to tell stories. Telling a story that adds value to the lives of Generation Y really works—and there are many stories associations could tell but don't. This generation is all about sharing, and there's plenty of scientific data to explain their sharing behaviors, the point being that experiences, photos, and products resonate with them.

Tell a story on Instagram or YouTube through photos and videos. Tell stories on your website. I'm not saying you should create a documentary here. Keep it brief and compelling and get to the point of how your association is making a difference in people's lives. Storytelling, authenticity, and uniqueness add more value than you might expect because they reflect Gen Y's core values and also support your association's brand and value proposition.

The National Retail Federation hosted a "This is Retail" video contest as a part of the association's multi-faceted Retail Means Jobs campaign. The winning video, which tells the story of how a retailer helped benefit cancer patients, received a $25,000 prize. The contest was designed to promote retail as a career and demonstrate the multitude of career choices available within the retail industry. The top 20 videos generated more than 420,000 online votes.

Exclusivity

The key here is to be inclusive with your marketing—inviting the participation of all age groups and skillsets—while being exclusive in the delivery of the experience. This is where membership associations have an advantage. By creating a coveted and unique experience available only to a small group of people (members), you will see the demand for your association's experiences increase. Associations that succeed at being both inclusive *and* exclusive pique interest, drive engagement, and generate sharing.

The Business Marketing Association (BMA) of Colorado started hosting behind-the-scenes events for its young professionals group (30 and under). Literally. The group met with the marketing team for the Denver Center for the Performing Arts, learning about how to market a show. The group then watched the show and had drinks with the cast afterwards.

Another popular event BMA hosted was limited to 30 people and hosted at a research facility that looked much like a home with couches and separate rooms. The 30 young professionals were broken into groups of 5–6 people and paired up with a notable CEO from the area. The small groups engaged in intimate discussions, then groups were asked to switch CEOs until they had met with each CEO.

Jonathan McGrew, the 29-year-old chair of the BMA young professionals, said the events have been successful because they provide access to people and places that members wouldn't otherwise have the opportunity to access. "These are people who are starting their careers, getting married, having kids, and working long hours. Their time is critical. We've got to find value adds that make sense for young professionals and we've got to be creative."

Interaction

Your association's website is more than just a billboard about your membership. Ditto for the Facebook page. Think of every interaction with your association as an experience and the visitors as your guests. Your website should embody your association's personality in a colorful, personal way. It should be organized, modern, and easy to navigate. Engage and connect with visitors on a deeper level with photos, videos, contests, infographics, and games.

Facebook can also enable interaction, inspiration, and community. Here are a few ideas: post updates on trending or controversial topics and ask followers to weigh in with their opinions, post snapshots from events, post an occasional comic or funny but relevant story, participate in Throwback Thursdays with historic pictures or trivia, randomly distribute prizes or shout-outs to followers, or invite followers to participate in photo and video contests. If you're only posting text-based status updates about an upcoming event you are missing a great opportunity to engage your audience.

Surprises

Share. Like. Post. Retweet. Marketers used to talk about publicity, buzz, and word-of-mouth marketing. Now social media terms are sitting front and center, but the concepts are the same: give people something to talk about. The element of surprise is effective and often overlooked. A surprise can be anything: bringing in a celebrity speaker at an event, sending members birthday cards, posting a video that no one has ever seen, recognizing an outstanding member or employee at random, showing up unexpectedly at a members place of business with balloons, lunch, or cake. Surprises create memorable experiences and get people talking, texting, and tweeting about your association.

Guts

When we're young, we really appreciate the trendy and extraordinary. Generation Y is no exception, and has in fact migrated from safety to adventure, as was explained in Chapter 2. This means that even as this generation ages, they have continued to gravitate towards travel and concerts, participate in color runs and other themed events, and more than 35 percent have tattoos. It can be argued that economic decline and being raised in a supervised environment has resulted in this generation's failure to launch—meaning they have delayed getting married and having children and have elongated the growing up process. In any case, Gen Ys are adventure-seekers and appreciate the organizations that have the guts to occasionally throw caution to the wind and live on the edge.

Credit Union Association of the Dakotas (CUAD) hosted a Harlem Shake video contest among members and also produced their own video, which generated lots of interest and laughs. Harlem Shake was an internet meme replicated by thousands in which people danced in costumes to electronica music. This is just the type of activity that will engage Generation Y. In a letter to the CUAD members, Kaitlyn Hardy, CUAD's Strategic Initiatives Specialist wrote: "I have learned firsthand just how challenging it is to attract the younger generation to our (credit union) movement. The Harlem Shake competition really demonstrated the fun and lighter side of our business. More importantly, it shows the fun and passion we all have for our respective credit unions as we successfully targeted younger members to our movement." The Huron branch of Dakotaland Federal Credit Union won the contest, for which CUAD awarded them a celebration pizza party.

Celebrities

While Generation Y seeks input from their peers, they will listen to high-profile individuals. They tend to have great relationships with their parents, and they tend to seek out these same relationships in their careers. This is why Generation Y will often request mentors. What they're really saying is they want access to, and an opportunity to learn from really successful individuals. Think of successful industry leaders as your association's in-house experts and celebrities. Try to get interviews or mentions on blogs written by them, or host a Twitter Chat with them. Bring in celebrity or high-profile speakers to your event and give members the opportunity to personally connect with them in a roundtable setting or Q & A opportunity. Access to the influential creates a great experience for members.

Nexstar Network surprised conference attendees with a photo shoot with Emmitt Smith, retired NFL running back. Attendees had the opportunity to get their photo taken with Smith after he keynoted Nexstar's annual conference. Using celebrities to draw in Generation Y can be a great experience for all members.

Marketing will never be the same again. Merely pushing advertising and creative positioning doesn't work anymore. Associations get so wrapped up in figuring out the frequency of their newsletters and what content to put in the members-only section of their websites.

None of that matters anymore. Nothing matters as much as your association's ability to forge a meaningful relationship with your audience, and those relationships are entirely based on your association's ability to create a great experience, ultimately making people feel smart, important, and happy. Audiences are driven almost entirely by emotion and experiences now, and there's scientific evidence to prove it.

Causes

The rise of the Experience Economy means Generation Y is inspired and motivated by emotions and experiences, so it makes perfect sense they would seek to engage in and support causes. It's common knowledge that Gen Y is looking for companies that make a difference globally as well as in their communities. They love affiliating with causes, but here again, few organizations take the extra effort to really understand why. Generation Y craves a relationship and needs to make a difference perhaps more than any other generation partly due to influences of their childhood and adolescence.

For starters, there's stress. A study commissioned by the American Psychological Association reveals this generation is the most stressed of all the generations. Of course, many people in this generation (21.6 millon Americans to be exact) are still living with their parents. This certainly explains the higher than average stress factor, right? At the time this book is being written only 6 in 10 Ys living in the United States have a job—and half of those jobs are part-time. Add to the fact that the average student loan debt as reported by The Project on Student Debt is $29,400 and you quickly understand why Generation Y is stressed.

Second, this generation has been raised amidst violence fairly close to home. Yes, they are the most protected and supervised generation, but the bike helmets and car seats haven't prevented the school shootings, Amber

Alerts, global warming, or September 11. These very near and present dangers, combined with the constant oversight of Helicopter Parents, has created a generation with an incredibly high desire for trustworthy, safe, transparent relationships.

Third, the influences of the Baby Boomer generation are apparent. The Boomers were raised to pursue the American Dream, and they've raised their children to also achieve, pursue their dreams, and to believe they are capable of accomplishing great things. As a result, Generation Y is inspired to change the world and believes they can make a difference.

COCA COLA

Staying relevant in a Generation Y-driven marketplace requires creativity, risk-taking, and constant reinvention. When Coca-Cola Chief Marketing and Commercial Officer Joe Tripodi presented at the Association of National Advertisers conference, he explained Coke is focused on innovation to keep pace with this altruistic, entrepreneurial, and tech-savvy generation.

Here are a few of the ways Coke is appealing to this generation:

- **Personalization**
  During the "Share a Coke" campaign, a promotion that launched in Australia, consumers could send their friends a Coke with their first name printed on the label. Sales spiked during the campaign, which has been replicated in 30 additional countries.

- **Provoking Happiness**
  Coca-Cola is moving from promoting happiness to provoking it through experiences that puts fans front-and-center. For example, Coke installed high-tech vending machines in two popular shopping malls in Lahore, Pakistan and New Delhi, India—two cities separated by only 325 miles but seemingly worlds apart due to decades of political tension. The "Small World Machines" used 3D touchscreen technology and video to capture a live emotional exchange between people in both countries. The machines encouraged people to complete a friendly task together—wave, touch hands, draw a peace sign or dance—before sharing a Coke. The interactive technology was especially appealing to Generation Y.

- **Positive Change**
  Generation Y expects companies like Coca-Cola to take a TAOS—Transparent, Authentic, Organic and Sustainable—approach to all communications. As a result, Coke wants to lead culture (not follow it) and be a voice that advocates for positive change. This includes supporting the Arctic Home campaign to save the polar bears and taking a leadership role in the obesity dialogue to offer low- and no-calorie beverages and encourage people to get active by supporting physical activity programs.

In 2010, amidst the Great Recession, Landor Associates conducted a survey to measure consumer perceptions. It found that despite the recession, nearly 50 percent of 18 to 24 and 25 to 34-year-olds who were surveyed were more likely to take a pay cut to work for a socially responsible company—a much higher percentage than any other age group.

The *Millennial Consumer,* a report published in 2012 by Boston Consulting Group, refers to the emergence of six key segments of the Gen Y consumer population—two of which are driven by social awareness:

- "Hip-ennials" want to make the world a better place. They are globally aware, charitable, and information hungry and comprise the largest segment of Gen Y consumers.

- "Clean and Green" Gen Ys are focused on green initiatives and concerned about taking care of the world. They are more likely to buy products that support sustainable farming or fair trade principles.

Generation Y is socially aware of the world around them and they frequently cite improving education, ending poverty, and saving the environment as their top concerns. This cause-driven mindset has propelled changes in existing businesses as well as start-ups. Associations that connect people to something bigger than themselves through their product or service will make a bigger impact with Generation Y.

One example of an association forging relationships through a cause is the National Christmas Tree Association, which donates free, real Christmas trees to military troops. This is a significant undertaking and a sacrifice, as these are quality, sellable trees being harvested, donated, and collected during the busiest possible time for tree growers. Members do it each year to bring joy to troops and their families. In 2013, 9,685 trees were donated by members.

Keith Greene, Chief Membership Officer at Meals On Wheels Association of America, says the Meals on Wheels cause has driven a younger audience to engage. The association has seen record numbers of volunteers and 25 percent of the association's volunteers are now under the age of 25. He noted that working with Gen Y "requires a lot of presence" because they want frequent communication and they are constantly connected and wanting to access more and more information.

Events for Generation Y

Events are planned experiences, but not all events are achieving the status of experiences as specified by the Experience Economy, which is based on having and delivering happiness.

We've all attended events that aren't especially memorable or may have even been disappointing, but the Experience Economy principles dictate attendees won't stand for mediocrity anymore. When an event comes to an end, the participants must revert back to normal life. An individual goes from a special state to an ordinary one. While attending the event, associations need people to feel a sense of community and change while they are there. Therefore, three things need to be present to create a meaningful experience: community (belonging); positive change (accomplishment or renewal); and happiness (escapism and appreciation). If attendees leave the event without feeling a sense of community, positive change, or happiness, then the experience was neither special nor memorable and they are less likely to return. It's the combination of these three concepts, which rely heavily on emotion, that drive people to attend events.

As I explained above, the emotions are what bring meaning to an experience. They enrich our lives and the feeling is addictive. It's the reason planned events exist in the first place. We seek to escape the ordinary and we crave unique experiences with others. As humans, we always have.

So why am I addressing the importance of creating exceptional experiences here? Because we've moved into an uber-competitive, time-starved society where time has literally become a commodity. This is especially true for Generation Y, an instant-gratification generation accustomed to multi-tasking and juggling jobs with volunteerism and personal time. Your association is competing for your members' time and attention all the time, and this is more obvious than ever with Generation Y. In the Experience Economy, everything your association does must deliver a meaningful experience or you're likely to see attendance and revenue take a sharp nosedive. Here are some examples of Experience Economy-designed events.

Red Bull: Community

After sponsoring a handful of existing events early in the brand's history, Red Bull made a strategic decision to create their own events and have followed this direction consistently ever since. Red Bull is fundamentally different in this regard, and really tapped into Generation Y's migration from safety to adventure. Most brands build recognition through product messaging, but Red Bull does it by creating experiences that generate tremendous publicity as well as a devoted fan-based community.

In fact, the Red Bull Flugtag (competitors attempt to fly home-made, human-powered flying machines) and Red Bull Soapbox Race are now yearly highlights, reaching in-person audiences of hundreds of thousands of people in many cities. In 2007 in Brazil, over one million people attended the Red Bull Air Race, a series of air races in which competitors have to navigate a challenging obstacle course in the fastest time.

Red Bull has made it their mission to bring barely imaginable experiences into existence, and give them all the spectacle and pomp of a real sporting event. They invest most of their budget in experiences, and that has built their brand and built a community of fans.

Gen Y loves Red Bull for its cool experiences, but also because the brand remains authentic. In fact, Red Bull's social media never inserts information about the energy drink itself. What you do see, over and over, are photographs of people doing remarkable things: surfing, snowboarding, car racing, skateboarding—and usually in some extreme manner. Red Bull's brand belongs entirely to its community of fans, entirely driven by experiences.

McDonald's: Positive Change for Others

There are two ways to act upon the positive change principle of the Experience Economy: creating an experience that allows attendees to create a positive change for self or an experience that creates a positive change for others.

The McDonald's Worldwide Convention created a positive change for others with the creation of a sustainability program capable of composting 84,000 pounds of food into livestock feed, donating 67,000 pounds of materials to local organizations, and diverting 71 percent of waste from landfills. The fast-food chain initiated the strategy at the biennial event beginning in 2008, and since then it has been developing new and innovative initiatives to create continuous improvement. McDonald's conveys the green message to the kids through programs offered at the convention's daily children's camp. The camp offers programs and field trips on health, wellness, and water and animal conservation.

Following the Worldwide Convention in Orlando, McDonald's donated conference materials to organizations around Central

Florida. Countertops and cabinets went to Habitat for Humanity, drapes went to a local theater group, and an entire marketplace exhibit went to a nearby fairgrounds. The McDonald's convention is relevant to Generation Y on many levels, meeting their values for making a difference, caring for the environment, and also providing a camp option for children of parents who want to attend the event.

TED: Positive Change for Self

The TED Conference is an example of an event creating positive change for self. TED is a global set of conferences owned by a nonprofit and devoted to a mission of exposing people to ideas worth spreading. This year (2014) TED celebrates its 30th anniversary. TED was born in 1984 out of Richard Saul Wurman's observation of a powerful convergence among three fields: technology, entertainment, and design.

For many attendees, TED became one of the intellectual and emotional highlights of the year. The principles that made TED great included the unique format of 18-minute talks, the breadth of content, and TED's commitment to seek out the most interesting people on earth and let them communicate their passion. Initially, attendees loved sharing in an exciting secret because TED was an invitation-only event.

Today, TED Conferences continue to inspire and motivate attendees and TED Talks are available online, averaging 17 new page views per second. TED has been an incredible success because attendees gain valuable knowledge and insight they can't easily get anywhere else. Plus, attendees are engaged intellectually and as a result they feel inspired, educated, and renewed.

In many ways TED was ahead of its time. It's especially relevant to Generation Y's style of learning. Gen Y loves the variety and quick access to information, the option to engage in-person or online, and the fact that TED continues to innovate. The brand continues to test new ways to create meaningful, engaging experiences for participants, such as at its hybrid gathering TEDActive.

At a 2013 TEDActive, the event featured a mix of seating options including theater seating, armchairs, beanbags, and even bed-style lounges. During the breaks, attendees were engaged in physical activities such as kite-flying and flag-making. The goal was to set the stage for conversations and audience engagement in a variety of ways. One of the conference's most popular engagement strategies, year after year, is the picnic lunch. Guests pick up a basket pre-packed with six lunches and are asked to find five other people with whom to share.

South by Southwest (SXSW): Happiness

The third principle of the Experience Economy is happiness, characterized by escapism and appreciation. This means that people engage in an experience because it provides them access to something really extraordinary (escapism) and something they really enjoy (appreciation). All the experiences mentioned up to this point serve up a healthy helping of happiness. Nevertheless, South by Southwest (SXSW) is one worth mentioning.

SXSW Music is the largest music festival of its kind in the world, with more than 2,200 official performers and bands playing in more than 100 venues. The event has grown from 700 registrants in 1987 to nearly 12,000 registrants. There are also the SXSW Film and SXSW Interactive events that are growing in popularity, as well.

In addition to discovering the latest and greatest trends and talent, SXSW fosters a culture of happiness that Generation Y loves and upon which the Experience Economy thrives. For example, SXSW featured a life-sized 1,000-foot-long track with Mario Karts modeled after the popular video game. The go-carts were equipped with GoPro cameras, which captured simulcasts on screens and sent them to individual drivers afterwards.

The photo-based marketing platform Together organized a selfie-contest at SXSW. Called SXSelfie, the campaign invited festival goers to submit mobile self-portraits to a dedicated website from which it displayed images at a party where attendees could vote on favorites. Those whose photos received the most votes became eligible to win a GoPro camera.

A music festival in and of itself makes people happy, and these additional experiences—focused on escapism and appreciation—makes the festival and participating brands all that more memorable.

Designing the Experience

Events aren't enough to capture people's attentions and hearts anymore. The chart below highlights some of the key differences between the old standard of hosting events and the new approach to creating experiences.

OLD: HOSTING EVENTS	NEW: CREATING EXPERIENCES
Interruption	Engagement
Reaction	Interaction
Attendees	Fans
Big promises	Personal gestures
Observers	Participants
Traditions	Innovation

The Experience Economy has changed the audience's expectations of events. When your association is considering the design of an experience, consider the following questions:

- **What would make your guests want to come in, sit down, and just hang out?**
  Think about how you can make the environment—the experience— more comfortable and inviting. You want to create an atmosphere in which your guests just feel free to be.

- **Once your guests are there, what do you want them to do?**
  I attended an event a few years ago and at one point there was a 45-minute lull in the action. Event organizers encouraged attendees to "take a break and network," but there wasn't any place designated for either activity. No chairs, no food, nothing. People ended up wandering off, going off-site or back to their hotel rooms. Just like that, 250 people disappeared! Focus on what you want guests to do if they are to engage, and create spaces that help them achieve your objectives for them.
  "We no longer use education rooms and Powerpoint. All of our education is on the trade show floor and most of it is developed in partnership with exhibitors and members," explained Emily Woody Bibens, CAE, and vice president of Woody Bibens and Associates, an association management company that manages the Western Nursery and Landscape Association. The association also booted its keynote

speakers. This has opened what Bibens refers to as "communication pathways" among attendees and Generation Y has the opportunity to engage in planning, leading, and interacting at the conferences.

- **What do you want guests to learn from the situation?**
No one wants to just sit and listen anymore. Think about interaction and activities that will help immerse the audience in the exploration of knowledge and skills. One example of this is digitalNow, an annual conference designed for the executive directors and senior-level leaders of associations. The conference promises to address the critical issues facing association leaders who are leading in the digital age and the entire event is focused on building relationships and the sharing of best practices executive-to-executive.

In addition to traditional keynote presentations, attendees are able to drill down to the application level with subject matter experts and business strategists—and even have an opportunity to speak one-on-one with leaders and experts in a variety of fields.

One of the conference highlights is the Fusion e.Comm.unity® Resource Center—a hands-on technology demonstration and learning area—where executives can talk to developers of some of the most innovative technologies in the association market in a completely sales-free environment. Unlike a trade show, the e.Comm.unity® provides an intimate consultation setting for executives to converse one-on-one with partners about innovations in products and services and based on relationship building.

"At this year's conference we'll be trying Google Glasses. At the first conference, I had access to Evernote (app designed for notetaking and archiving) while it was still in beta. Everything about this conference focuses on innovation and driving the future of associations forward," stated Danielle Marshall, chief strategy officer at Consulting Management Innovators.

- **What entertainment would help your guests enjoy the experience?**
When your guests are entertained, they're positively responding to the experience. Making an experience fun and enjoyable is really valuable. For Synergos' fraternity and sorority association clients, Mark Koepsell, CAE, said they go for a rock conference feel. Loud music, big screens, videos—it's all about the cool factor with this audience. The events also appeal to different learning styles, mixing up theater with interactive presentations. The conference is produced

much like a TED Conference, going for high-tech, professionally produced, and what Koepsell refers to as "icing on the cake moments." There are "competition" conferences, costing about $75–$100 less but Koepsell says students are willing to pay more because of the experience this conference provides.

Walt Disney came up with the idea for Disneyland because he didn't think the fairground experience was all that great. He wanted his daughters to experience something better. There are two lessons to be learned here. One is finding opportunity to create a new, better, and more relevant experience. The other is that Disneyland is concerned with being the happiest place on earth for all generations today—but it was originally created with the youngest generation in mind.

CHAPTER 7

Rocking the Vote

*"Young professionals are feeling very disenfranchised
with government. We don't want to get involved, but the
fact is associations need their involvement. It's important
for our collective futures. So try to make it meaningful,
interesting, and even fun. Take the scary out of advocacy
and my generation will start to pay attention."*

Ashley Hodak Sullivan
Chief Operating Officer
New York State Trial Lawyers Association
Age: 28

Impact Economy

Sir Richard Branson, billionaire entrepreneur and founder of the
Virgin Group, has signed a declaration. Not unlike the Declaration of
Independence, it may very well mark a change in our collective futures.
In the declaration, Branson and several other notable business leaders
pledge to "focus on ourselves, our own businesses and industries, and do
our utmost to ensure we meet the principles of better business." This is the
Declaration of The B Team. Co-founded and launched in 2013 by Branson,
The B Team is so named because Plan B is an alternative to the current
Plan A of business driven solely by a profit motive.

Evidently, Plan A isn't really working the way Branson and others
had hoped. Plan B is a tall order of intentions and The B Team leaders
have put their leadership on the line calling for a new way of doing
business. Thus far, we've explored how Generation Y's coming of age
has contributed to the emergence of four new economies—the Sharing,
Knowledge, Gig, and Experience economies. The fifth and final economy
is the Impact Economy. The Impact Economy is one that promotes social,
environmental, as well as economic value creation—exactly what The
B Team is advocating for and trying to achieve.

The B Team website invites the participation of a global community to
work on accelerating Plan B for a world "in which the purpose of business
is to be a driving force for social, environmental and economic benefit."

During this time of mounting fiscal challenges and a sluggish and fragile economic recovery, there is a growing sector of for-benefit enterprises that have emerged to create quality jobs, promote economic growth, contribute to the tax base, drive new resources to the nonprofit sector, and tackle a wide range of social and environmental issues that would otherwise fall on the shoulders of government and nonprofits. Before I delve into how the Impact Economy will change advocacy for associations, I think it's best to demonstrate how the Impact Economy actually came into being.

The Big Global Crack-Up

Remember when associations and other membership organizations, like Rotary and chambers of commerce, enjoyed a lock on their markets? The Baby Boomers joined associations in droves. Now, participation is changing, fueled by social changes, generational shifts, a recession-prone economy, and rapidly changing technology. In 2011 I authored a book on this very conundrum: *The End of Membership as We Know It* (ASAE: The Center for Association Leadership).

While I've spent a great deal of time in recent years researching changing demographics and changing membership models and educating people on these topics, it's important to note change is happening on a substantial scale with radical proportions everywhere—in every industry and every country all over the world. Absolutely everything about the way everyone lives, works, and conducts business is changing. Welcome to the Impact Economy.

In 2011, Thomas Friedman, author and *New York Times* foreign affairs columnist, wrote a column addressing the substantial change that's taking place on a global level.

> The European Union is cracking up. The Arab world is cracking up. China's growth model is under pressure and America's credit-driven capitalist model has suffered a warning heart attack and needs a total rethink. Recasting any one of these alone would be huge. Doing all four at once—when the world has never been more interconnected—is mind-boggling.

Indeed, 2011 was a turning-point year. Several dictators were overthrown, including Egypt's Hosni Mubarak, in power since 1981; Libya's Muammar Gaddafi, prime minister for 42 years; Ivory Coast's Laurent Gbagbo whose refusal to leave spawned violent civil conflict; and Yemen's Ali Abdullah Saleh who had ruled since 1978. This was also the year U.S. Navy Seals found and executed Osama bin Laden, leader of the Islamist militant group, al-Qaeda.

Friedman cited the following additional examples to support his global cracking up diagnosis in 2011:

- European countries with large government welfare programs and no revenue to finance them from local production, led to a piling up of sovereign debt and a lender revolt;

- The old model of power based on kings and military dictators in the Middle East was blown apart by an Arab youth bulge no longer ready to accept being behind, undereducated, unemployed, humiliated, and powerless;

- Persistent unemployment in China made its Communism model—featuring a deliberately undervalued currency and export-led growth—less sustainable and fallen under threat; and

- America's credit-consumption-led economy resulted in a recession and the emergence of new, hybrid politics mixing spending cuts, tax increases, tax reform, and investments in education, research and production.

Yes, 2011 was a year marked by political and economic shift, and I would argue those shifts were largely spawned by demographic shifts and one generation's not-so-gracious fall from power.

I agree with Mark Goulston, Vice Chairman of Steele Partners, who authored an opinion column for *The Huffington Post* in response to Friedman's column citing demographic shifts as the real reason for the global crack up:

> When you read Friedman's column about the institutions of various countries, continents and cultures of the world, it appears that they are breaking down as the younger generations globally are seeing what others have, and how others live, and how they could have and live the same. Friedman doesn't say it explicitly, but if you read between his lines and then look around you at the different generations, you will see that a revolution is brewing. But it is not brewing between democratic and totalitarian regimes. It is between generations.

So what does all this mean to your association and its advocacy efforts? It means Generation Y isn't accepting of the status quo. It means this generation isn't accustomed to, or even comfortable with, the idea that advocacy and government can solve people's problems. It means Generation Y isn't going to engage in advocacy the same way previous generations have engaged. It means your association may also need a Plan B.

I'm not saying advocacy isn't relevant anymore, but it certainly has evolved. Here are a few additional insights to further demonstrate why it isn't—and can't be—politics as usual with this generation.

- **The United States has the oldest Congress in history and the oldest Senate in more than a century.** Elected officials are aging and Generation Y isn't especially interested in running for office or participating in advocacy efforts. Central to the problem in the United States is our reliance on 18th-century electoral laws, 19th-century party models, and 20th-century systems of political communication. Currently there is one Gen Y in Congress and there isn't a Gen Y in the Senate. According to research conducted by First Person Politics, Generation Y won't comprise the majority in the House of Representatives until around 2035 or the Senate until sometime between 2036 and 2044. The Boomers became the majority in 1995.

- **This generation is rejecting public service as a career path.** As Baby Boomers approach retirement, the U.S. federal government will need to hire more than 200,000 highly skilled workers for a range of critical jobs. Presently, the nation's government is staring down a brain drain of unfathomable magnitude. Just 6 percent of college students plan to work for public sector institutions, and only 2.3 percent want to work at the federal level. Generation Y has no patience for inefficiency, stodgy institutions or the status quo, and they want results—all reasons why they are disengaging from public service and government work.

- **A whopping 43 percent of the world's population is under the age of 25.** Political and government officials are aging, but the majority population is getting younger. This has already had, and will continue to have, a profound influence on future policy at national, regional, and global levels. For example, U.S. President Barack Obama's election and reelection were attributed to capturing Gen Y's vote. Political analysts cited that ignoring the youth vote was the downfall in the campaigns of both John McCain and Mitt Romney. In 2012, some 61 to 66 percent of Gen Y voted for Obama in the swing states of Ohio, Florida, Pennsylvania, and Virginia.

- **Generation Y doesn't see politics or government as a way to improve their communities, their country, or the world.** Contrary to popular belief, Generation Y does vote. In fact, young voter turnout has been steadily increasing since 2004—tracking at the highest turnouts since 1972. There was likely a moment when Obama was elected that the case could have been made to Generation Y that government is transcendent. They loved the concepts of hope and change that Obama touted. Their enthusiasm has since subsided, coming of age in a period of polarization and gridlock, which the president they supported could not overcome. In a 2014 Pew Research Center survey, about half of Generation Y said the president failed to change the way Washington works. According to the Survey of Young Americans' Attitudes Toward Politics and Public Service, some 47 percent agree that "politics today are no longer able to meet the challenges our country is facing" and 51 percent believe that government is wasteful and inefficient.

- **Advocacy is an opportunity.** Generation Y has wielded their power in elections and political revolutions the world over, but associations have failed to engage them in advocacy. In 2013, XYZ University conducted an advocacy-focused study of 125 membership associations. The study revealed that while 83 percent of the associations promoted advocacy as a primary member benefit and reason for members to join the association, only 12 percent were actually engaging Generation Y in advocacy efforts and activities. According to the *Associations Matter: 2013 State of the Sector Report* of Australian associations, only 6 percent of respondents' (from all age groups) rated advocacy services as a reason for joining.

Clearly, Generation Y is powerful. And amidst demographic shifts and rising economies, we're being forced to rethink what advocacy is and how it works. One thing is certain: associations can't continue to focus on selling advocacy as a member benefit. Advocacy is meaningless to this generation and riddled with negativity. Nevertheless, associations should take solace in the fact that advocacy isn't dead. It remains meaningful, important, and relevant but has been completely redefined. Generation Y might not be interested in advocacy, but they are definitely activists.

A Generation of Activists Emerges

Up until now, America's political system has largely neglected its succession planning efforts, overlooked the relevance of engaging younger generations, and dismissed them for their youthful tendencies and stereotyped them as disinterested and difficult to reach. Is it really any surprise that Generation Y isn't jumping on any political bandwagons?

Now faced with such a significant shift in demographics, our political and community leaders are realizing the error of their ways. Writing younger generations off politically was a mistake, and we must find a way to re-engage them and prepare them to take over the reins.

Just as associations have struggled without the engagement of younger generations, our government and political arenas are experiencing the same fate. We can't rely or survive on the participation of one generation in these new economies. If this book proves nothing else, it should prove the value and importance of collaboration, leadership, innovation, and engagement of every generation in every organization.

William Galston, a former policy advisor to President Clinton has written about the departure of young Americans from the electorate. He wrote: "The withdrawal of a cohort of citizens from public affairs disturbs the balance of public deliberation—to the detriment of those who withdraw, but of the rest of us as well." Michael Slaby, Chief Technology Officer for the Obama Campaign who is now the Chief Technology Strategist for TomorrowVentures, LLC echoed this concern. "The more engaged and informed the electorate is as a whole, the better democracy works as a whole," he stated. In other words, in order for democracy to work at its best, every sector of society must be engaged in political life.

By 2015 young people ages 18–29 will make up one third of the voting population. They are the future electorate—and regardless of whose fault it is, young Americans are simply not engaged. At least that's what we think is happening because we only measure engagement in traditional ways in established organizations. If we take a broader view, we can see this generation of activists is very engaged, blazing new trails, and in hot pursuit of their mission to change the world.

Social Enterprise

To Gen Y, the world is filled with injustice and need, but government isn't the solution. They may be less radical than their Baby Boomer parents, whose demonstrations for civil rights, women's equality, and protests against the Vietnam War became flashpoints for their times. Still, the apple didn't fall far from the tree. Generation Y wants to change the world, and they are much more aware of the world because of their access to technology.

Generation Y was born into a world already defined by historic shifts like the women's movement, the spread of political freedoms and access to education, and the growth of middle classes in many developing countries. They haven't known oppression and they've been raised to believe they have the capacity to do anything—including being a change-maker.

At the same time, Generation Y was born into a technology-driven information revolution. They are accustomed to the rapid pace of change, the concept of instant gratification, and they have always been highly aware of the fact that institutions—especially governments and businesses—are failing to address big problems in the environment, the economy, and education.

This generation has come of age during the Iraq War and War on Afghanistan and has observed several tragedies close to home, such as the 9/11 terrorist attacks, global warming, Amber Alerts, suicides, school shootings, and Hurricane Katrina. This is a generation concerned about global warming, who broadly supports equality for the lesbian-gay-bisexual-transgender (LGBT) community, has no qualms about interracial marriage, and are much more diverse and civic-minded than other generations.

Put all these influences together—a world rocked by change, faced daily with new information and threats to survival, and a stalled government—and you get a generation who believes the only way to improve the situation is by innovation and taking matters into its own hands.

That's why Generation Y is more likely to be social entrepreneurs working for social enterprises, meaning they prefer to work outside government to create innovative and measurably successful solutions to the nation's problems. The terms "social enterprise" and "social entrepreneur" means this generation engages in collaborative problem solving (social) and takes the initiative to make a positive change (entrepreneurship) or works for a company that seeks to make positive social change (enterprise).

Gen Y believes in social entrepreneurship, meaning they think they can do well both financially and for the world around them. For example:

- 56 percent would take a pay cut to work somewhere that is positively changing the world (The Cassandra Good Guide, 2012);

- 85 percent make purchasing decisions based on a company's link to causes (*Millennial Momentum* book, 2011);

- 81 percent donated money, goods, or services—even during the recession (Walden University and Harris Interactive, 2011);

- More than two thirds believe that they could make more of a difference in the world by running their own business than they could by running for political office (The Cassandra Good Guide, 2012).

When Pew Research asked a sample of Gen Ys what their top priorities were, they said being a good parent, having a successful marriage, and helping others in need.

As social entrepreneurs, Gen Y pursues opportunities to solve the world's problems, while continuously adapting and learning and drawing upon appropriate thinking in both the business and nonprofit worlds. They also believe that businesses should focus on a societal purpose, not just be in business to make a profit. This is why you see so many Gen Ys become social entrepreneurs or support their local nonprofit—they always need to feel like they are making a difference, regardless of their job title.

The same is true for your association. Generation Y is going to expect your association to focus on a greater good and to engage members in the process. Just being a member to further your network or skills won't be enough for this generation.

Today, as problems have grown increasingly complex, the big question is how can the problem-solving work of society be redesigned so it is more responsive to needs. Hence, advocacy is changing.

Three generations ago, the federal government could address many forms of injustice through legislation—mandating a 40-hour workweek, instituting a minimum wage, establishing housing codes. Today, our societal challenges in education, health, or the environment demand innovation from many directions, and a faster response.

The fact is, the capacity and motivation needed to solve problems is now widely dispersed. Associations have access to some of the best talent and ideas among thousands—even millions—of people. Advocacy can't be about motivating people to send letters to elected officials anymore. Associations must think like social entrepreneurs and find ways to elicit, nurture, and harness the talents of millions of potential change-makers for a greater good. Here's insight to the way a social enterprise works.

Build a Movement, not Market Share

Associations that are thinking like social enterprises won't just want to sell more memberships; they will want to change a whole industry. That means thinking about how to turn your association into a movement so that the impact can go far beyond benefitting a small group of members and far beyond just your association's reach.

Consider the example of VisionSpring. Jordan Kassalow is the founder of this social enterprise on a mission to bring affordable eyeglasses to low-income, visually impaired people everywhere. Shortly after VisionSpring sold its first million eyeglasses, Kassalow realized that with 700 million visually impaired people in the developing world, he needed to do more; he needed to build a global movement.

First, VisionSpring trained 20,000 sales agents and is now closing in on 2 million customers—500,000 of whom were reached in 2013 alone. Still, Kassalow isn't satisfied. In 2014, he met with numerous leaders of influence including leaders from the United Nations, MasterCard, British Telecom, Amazon, and the Gates Foundation among many others. Kassalow's goal is to inform influencers of his mission—especially influencers in those organizations where vision is important to success in learning, working, and safety.

Kassalow wrote about his quest to connect important people with the important issue he's trying to solve. He explained that in order to move from building an enterprise to building a movement, it would take a dedicated mix of people from government, the private sector, and civil society.

Another example of a social entrepreneur is Blake Mycoskie. In 2006 he visited Argentina and was struck by the intense poverty and lack of shoes for children. He created TOMS shoes, a company that would donate one pair of shoes to a child in need for every pair that was sold.

The motto of this multi-million dollar company to "be in business to help change lives" has resonated with Gen Y. They respect TOMS as a brand that is aware of what is going on in the world and making it a better place. In 2013, TOMS hit a milestone—donating more than 10 million shoes in just 7 years.

Social entrepreneurs and enterprises focus on achieving social change through relationships, and this change isn't reliant on money and it actively welcomes competition.

If your organization really wants to succeed in the Impact Economy, you need more than a sales plan and a profit motive—you need a mission. Mission, not money, has emerged as the greatest motivator of people. Some refer to this as "empathetic capitalism," which is the development of a values-driven business where money is the enabler but not the motivator.

In social enterprise, competition is good because it means there are more people trying to solve the problem. Social enterprise also thrives on Digital Activism, where sharing, liking, tweeting, hashtagging, and re-blogging are just as valued as taking to the streets. This aligns well with Generation Y's cause-related bracelets and likes for causes on Facebook.

Associations are familiar with some of these principles but not others. From building major league baseball stadiums to getting legislation passed that protects hundreds of businesses from closure, I'm familiar with several examples of associations using advocacy for good. However, there are some key differences between social entrepreneurs like Kassalow and advocacy in associations—practices that associations would benefit from adopting.

This chart helps to explain some of the differences between social entrepreneurs and advocacy.

SOCIAL ENTREPRENEURS	ADVOCACY
Action-based. Identifies a problem and gives people an immediate opportunity to create or contribute to the solution.	**Information-based.** Identifies a problem, proposes a new solution, and communicates with evidence.
Purpose-driven. A diverse audience gives their support and finances for social good.	**Profit-driven.** Member companies pay dues to support representation at the Capital.
Grassroots. Engages many people across a broad community in promoting and creating a significant, sustained change.	**Watchdog.** Informs a small group with intent to mobilize them in advocating for an urgent or specific change.
Relationship-based. Builds a following organically through trust, ethics, fairness, and trusted relationships.	**Research-based.** Builds awareness intentionally based on the dissemination of research, data, or specific facts.
Digital. Encourages sharing, liking, tweeting, hashtagging, and re-blogging.	**Traditional.** Encourages email and letter writing, faxing, fly-ins, and meetings.
Constant. Communicates outcomes and purpose through a variety of mediums, messages, and people year-round.	**Episodic.** Alerts a specific audience on urgent issues via targeted communications while Congress is in session.
Growing. Committed to growth and open to competition to benefit more people and do more social good. Number of participants and causes continues to increase.	**Declining.** Committed to the preservation of an industry or occupation. Number of participants engaging in advocacy efforts continues to decline.

As you can see, advocacy in its current format differs from social enterprise. Social enterprise is emerging and growing as Generation Y shows and shares their social consciousness through the products they choose, the entertainment they consume, and the activities they pursue.

This generation, raised during and assuming leadership of the Impact Economy, could rescue the civic health of our nation—and the world for that matter—because they are products of an era of economic crisis and war and they are so committed to community service. Gen Ys really believe it is on them to make positive change in the world. In fact, when asked who the person is who is most capable of making a difference in the world, they only ranked the President ahead of themselves.

While the active participation of Baby Boomers and older generations is excellent, we cannot continue along this path of dominance on one end of the age spectrum and inactivity on the other end. Generation Y's participation (or lack thereof) could determine America's political landscape and policies for many years to come.

Why bother with outreach to younger generations? For three critical reasons:

1. America is on the brink of the largest turnover in human capital in history and even though the voting majority is getting younger, America's political representatives are getting older.

2. The young vote counts now more than ever before. Even if they turn out at lower rates, today's young voting population is so large they can dramatically affect the election landscape and outcomes.

3. The participation of young, motivated people has the potential to revitalize America's federal, state, and city governments. Revitalization would likely be good considering the current state of America's political affairs: partisanship and political gridlock has become the norm; the nation has an accumulating trillion-dollar budget deficit; and the United States has been at war in Iraq or Afghanistan since 2003.

In the current political climate of scandals, heightened partisan discourse, and a struggling economy, politics is a challenge few young people are willing to tackle. Young people feel frustrated, powerless, distrusting, fearful, and disconnected.

Generational disengagement in politics and elsewhere is usually the direct result of one of three things:

1. Feeling powerless to make a difference;
2. Feeling there is no room to get involved; or
3. Feeling uninformed.

In the political arena, all of these barriers are currently present, yet one candidate was able to overcome these challenges and win the favor of Generation Y.

Targeting Gen Y

In 2008, Barack Obama's energized presidential campaign turned out about 15 million voters who went to the polls for the first time. Many of these first-time voters were young, female, minority, and independent—unaffiliated with any political party. In the end, Obama received 66 percent of Generation Y's vote.

Many people believed young people related to Barack Obama simply because he was young himself. However, he is the fifth youngest president, inaugurated at 47 years old. For a recent comparison, Bill Clinton was 46 years old when he was inaugurated in 2001. Theodore Roosevelt, John F. Kennedy, and Ulysses S. Grant assumed office at 42, 43, and 46 respectively. The difference was that Obama intentionally targeted the younger population. In fact, on many levels the Obama campaign far surpassed any volunteer movement in political history.

Regardless of party affiliation, there's no denying that Obama's campaign was a hit with young voters. There are lessons to be learned here. What did this candidate do differently? Here's a list of just a few differentiators:

- **Focus and Reach.** Obama was the first candidate to be marketed like a high-end brand. His campaign launched with a logo similar to Pepsi's logo, a call to action (Change We Can Believe In), a sophisticated recruitment and mobilization effort to target young voters on and off college campuses, and an aggressive marketing campaign utilizing YouTube, Facebook, MySpace, text messaging, and cell phones to reach young voters. Among the first apps for Apple's new iPhone was an Obama "Countdown to Change" calendar ticking off the seconds until Election Day.

- **Training and Support.** While all campaigns rely heavily on volunteers to carry the candidate's message and do much of the grunt work, the Obama campaign tried something different with Camp Obama. The Camp, designed for students and young adults (Generation Y), featured four-day training sessions designed to hone the political skills of young volunteers and teach them the basics of organizing for a presidential candidate. Camp Obama provided participants with the needed training and tools to create a campaign plan. Camp directors also kept in touch with campers after camp to provide support and help them execute their strategies.

- **Selective Search and Skill Development.** The Obama campaign offered Fellowships, which was a volunteer drive to find the best and brightest volunteers. Applicants were required to answer essay questions, supply references, and go through a telephone interview with campaign staff members. In return for a promise to give the campaign at least six weeks of full-time political work, volunteers were promised training in community-organizing techniques. More than 10,000 people applied. In the end, some 3,600 volunteers were deployed in 17 states.

- **Recognition.** During the course of his presidential campaign, Barack Obama often highlighted his volunteers at rallies. At many events, he chose one of them—rather than a local politician—to introduce him.

- **Online Outreach.** The Obama campaign created its own social-networking site, called my.barackobama.com (MyBO for short). The site encouraged visitors to take some kind of action to help the campaign, such as organizing a small party and downloading campaign literature to hand out to friends and neighbors. Once you gave the campaign your e-mail address, you would receive messages, sometimes signed by Michelle Obama or former Vice President Al Gore. These messages would ask people to perform specific functions helpful to the campaign. The campaign also rallied people based on geography, providing MyBO members with lists of people living nearby who were not registered to vote and instructions for contacting and registering them. Thanks to MyBO—plus other strategies, including asking people at rallies to text message their e-mail addresses to the campaign—Obama developed a huge group of online volunteers. According to America.gov, when the campaign ended, Obama held a list of 13 million supporters and their e-mail addresses. This was an enormous and unprecedented achievement.

- **Expert Advice.** Obama worked with Chris Hughes, then 25 years old, co-founder of Facebook, in order to leverage social networking to reach Generation Y. He also brought in other Gen Ys to work on the campaign and lead initiatives focused on reaching that generation.

If anything can be learned from the unprecedented success of the Obama campaign's volunteer movement, it's that young people are an emerging, capable, and very powerful demographic that should not be overlooked. "Generation Y holds strong values and strong intent," notes Stefanie Reeves, MA and CAE, Senior Legislative and Federal Affairs Officer, American Psychological Association. "They are willing to be a part of your movement, your advocacy, so long as they see the benefit to society and the benefit to them. Engage your younger members by engaging with them through their interests, their passions and their causes." Reeves said the American Psychological Association has experienced success with engaging Generation Y by thinking of ways to make advocacy informative, engaging, and inclusive of them.

For example, the association utilizes social media and directs Gen Ys to the Facebook pages or Twitter handles of the members of Congress who are champions for the association's issues. The association invites Gen Y to serve on the government relations committee and keeps the budgets of young people in mind when it comes to promoting the PAC, opening up the option for donating $25 or $50. APA also organizes a Hill Day for college students featuring advocacy training and a networking reception.

"Associations need to figure out a way to engage all members across generations in their advocacy efforts in order to be successful," Reeves noted. She said many associations make the mistake of tailoring all their advocacy efforts to Boomers.

"There's no excuse for excluding your younger members from your grassroots advocacy. Some of the best Hill visits I've ever sat in on were with our students and new professionals. They brought a passion to their meetings with congressional staff that some of our veterans can't match."

Predicting the future of U.S. government is challenging, but this much is certain: The government in existence today isn't engaging or relevant to the future majority; sooner or later, change won't just be a campaign slogan anymore. It will become a reality.

Call to Action

Unprecedented changes are occurring and we must be responsive to them. I recommend association leaders take an active role in succession planning for the benefit of their advocacy efforts but also for the sustainability of our nation's government. Just as associations have the relationships and opportunities to influence change in the business world, they have the potential to influence change in the political arena as well.

By 2015, Generation Y will make up one third of potential voters. This generation will want candidates who are genuine, honest, and visionary—exactly the characteristics they seek in every leader and organization as a generation of social entrepreneurs and activists. Associations need to take this demand to heart as they design the advocacy programs and efforts relevant to this next generation.

A disturbing statistic is that more than half of our nation's top elected officials were holding an office by the time they were 35 years old. How many 35 year olds do you know in office today? The trend of young Americans running for office has ceased. There is a significant lack of young people elected to office—or running for office—both nationally and locally. Associations can help to change this.

Our nation needs organizations to take a vested interest in advocating for more young people to run for office and also provide them with the information, tools, and support to be able to do so.

Beginning in the 1980s, civics requirements in high schools were gradually reduced. As of 2009, only 21 states included civic learning in their state assessment and accountability systems. Rock the Vote is taking matters into their own hands with Democracy Class. Through this free and non-partisan class, high school students nationwide will learn about the history of voting, the connection between issues they care about and those they elect to office, and their right to vote. The supporting website, DemocracyClass.com, offers access to election information, ways to get involved in registering voters, interviews with artists and athletes, and materials for teachers and community groups to use in their classrooms. All in an attempt to garner more interest with Generation Y in local and national governments.

The fact is, if your association wants to engage Generation Y in advocacy, your association is going to need to create a process that's relevant to Generation Y, and the association will likely need to help them understand why your advocacy efforts are needed and exactly how they can be an important contributor to those efforts.

As ambitious and successful young adults begin their careers and families, we need everyone—regardless of party affiliation—to understand, support, and engage in our nation's political system. Not someday, but in the near future. Our democracy depends on it. To borrow from the words of Thomas Jefferson, "Every generation needs a new revolution." Undoubtedly, change in the political arena is this generation's revolution. It's their Plan B, which means your association needs a Plan B, too.

CHAPTER 8

Getting Y to Work

"Nonprofits aren't talking to younger generations about career opportunities. I never even considered the world of nonprofits as an option. I wasn't even aware of it. It wasn't until someone told me about an association, and I joined, that I realized this was the place for me. Now I have a master's degree and my career aspirations are totally in this sector."

Michael Nevergall
Associate Vice President, Development
Lutheran Social Services of the South
Age: 30

During most of the 20th century Kodak held a dominant position in photographic film, and in 1976, had an 89 percent market share of photographic film sales in the United States. Kodak began to struggle financially in the late 1990s as a result of the decline in sales of photographic film and its slowness in transitioning to digital photography. In 2012, the company filed for Chapter 11 bankruptcy protection. The company is now trying to rebuild and rebrand itself as a digital printing and technology company.

While the Kodak name has become synonymous with a resistance to change, it's not just innovation that Kodak lacked. In 2011, Kodak made the list of Top 10 Fortune 500 Employers With Older Workers. With 38 percent of its workforce over the age of 50, Kodak was called out for employing a disproportionately high percentage of mature workers. Only American Airlines scored higher, coming in at 39 percent.

I can't help but wonder: If Kodak had paid attention to its aging workforce trend, focused on bringing in younger talent and diversifying its workforce—would the company have maintained market share and avoided bankruptcy? And herein lies the rub: Associations are nearing the danger zone when it comes to aging workforce demographics as well.

In fact, according to the U.S. Bureau of Labor Statistics, the category "Membership Associations and Organizations" is currently the nation's 14th-oldest industry by median employee age, clocking in with an average age of 48.6 years old. To be more specific, associations rank 14th out of 322 industries, which places them among the top 5 percent of the oldest industries in America.

Thus far, this book has addressed Generation Y from a membership perspective, but I would be remiss if I didn't also mention associations need to be concerned about engaging this generation as employees, too. Not only that, but if associations can help their member companies do the same, they will be sitting on a goldmine of opportunity.

There's an urgent, global need to reinvest in the next generation of employees and leaders. Unfortunately, the recession prolonged the natural progression that usually occurs in the workforce, making it easy for organizations to put the retirement wave on the backburner and not worry about it boiling over.

But the recession didn't stop people from aging. As a result, Generation Y—the largest generation in history who's been forced to wait on the sidelines—will also be unprepared to move into positions of responsibility and leadership. Although the recession ended in the summer of 2009, five years later unemployment for Generation Y remains near its cyclical peak across the globe.

In Britain, they are NEETS—not in education, employment, or training. In Japan, they are freeters: an amalgam of the English word freelance and the German word *Arbeiter,* or worker. Spaniards call them mileuristas, meaning they earn no more than 1,000 euros a month. In the United States, they're the boomerang generation who live with their parents because they can't find work. In 2010, CNN reported a whopping 85 percent of graduating college seniors in the United States were moving back home. Even fast-growing China, where labor shortages are more common than surpluses, has its ant tribe—recent college graduates who crowd together in cheap flats on the fringes of big cities because they can't find well-paying work.

According to the Organization for Economic Cooperation and Development (OECD), Generation Y is facing record unemployment levels in many countries, with rates exceeding 60 percent in Greece, 52 percent in South Africa, 55 percent in Spain, and around 40 percent in Italy and Portugal.

In each of these nations, an economy that can't generate enough jobs to absorb its young people has created a lost generation of the disaffected, unemployed, or underemployed. While the details differ from one nation to the next, the common element is failure—not just of young people to find a place in society, but of society itself to harness the energy, intelligence, and enthusiasm of the next generation. With no place to go, the largest, best-educated generation in history has become an under-utilized resource. Generation Y's unemployment is quite possibly the least understood and worst economic disaster of our time.

In the most-developed nations, the job market has split between high-paying jobs that many Gen Y workers aren't qualified for and low paying jobs that they can't live on. Many of the jobs that once paid good wages to high school graduates have been automated or outsourced. In other cases, employers have a preference for hiring senior citizen or immigrant workers because they tend to accept lower wages than youth and young professionals.This probably isn't news to you or to anyone else. Everyone seems to be aware of the problem; they just aren't doing anything about it.

In media reports on the topic Britain's Employment Minister refers to chronic unemployment as a "ticking time bomb," and Giuliano Amato, former Prime Minister of Italy laments "The older generations have eaten the future of the younger ones." Jeffrey Joerres, chief executive officer of Manpower, warns that unemployment among the youngest generation will become the "epidemic" of the next decade. There are plenty of warning signs, notable leaders, and media mentions addressing the topic. Yet, little has been done to move our companies and countries in a different direction.

About 40 years ago, shortly after the Boomers were born and the generation that followed was significantly smaller by comparison, demographers and industry leaders realized that someday the Boomers would retire and the nation would experience a shortage of experienced and knowledgeable talent.

Alas, the time has come. We're on the brink of the largest shift in human capital in history and we're still not prepared. The U.S. Census Bureau and Bureau of Labor Statistics predict Generation Y will become the majority of the workforce by 2015, and make up a staggering 75 percent of the global workplace in 2025. It's high time—in fact, it might be too late—to start preparing for and developing the next generation of talent.

My question is this: Why aren't associations taking the lead?

Associations are uniquely perched at the forefront of industries, frequently intersecting with government and education, and watching this entire talent crisis unfold. Associations have the knowledge, connections, and influence so desperately needed to solve the workforce crisis, yet they remain stuck. Like Kodak, they are unable to engage younger generations themselves, so they remain vastly incapable of adapting to the sea of change taking place around them. Up to this point, some associations have chosen to be part of the problem instead of being part of the solution. That has to change.

Workforce Development

Workforce development for Generation Y is desperately needed in three key areas, and associations can take an influential role in each. In the book *A+ Solution* (2013), the authors make the case how and why associations are perfectly positioned to effectively and efficiently train and support the workforce. Unemployment is the most pressing issue. We have an entire generation with minimal work experience vastly unprepared to move into positions of influence or power and pick up where the Boomers leave off. This naturally leads to the need for skill development and leadership development.

It's important to note that even with jobs, Gen Y isn't financially secure. Throughout my research I encountered several college-educated young professionals who were juggling more than one job to make ends meet or working especially long hours to try to impress their bosses and earn a promotion. For a number of reasons ranging from financial need to a lack of challenge to changing workforce dynamics, Generation Y is also the generation with the highest volume of employee turnover.

While associations may not be able to eradicate the workforce development crisis, they can certainly take a more active role and make a positive change for companies, industries, and entire nations. Here are a few ways associations can get Generation Y to work.

Unemployment

Young adult unemployment is tempting to dismiss. After all, the young have their whole lives ahead of them. They have fewer obligations and time is on their side considering they are young, healthy, and have several years to save for retirement. That all may be true, but the problem with this theory is that it doesn't take the economy into consideration. Generation Y will become the majority of the workforce as early as 2015. If the youngest, best educated, and largest talent pool struggles, the entire economy struggles.

Coming of age in a recession makes it difficult for this generation to quickly bounce back. There's accumulating student loan debt, bills, and increasing responsibilities and stress. The longer Gen Y is down and out, the longer it will take to get them on their feet. So it's important to look at the big picture here. Unemployment among Generation Y affects *every* generation. It's the Trickle-Up Effect at work once again. That's why employers (associations included) should be more concerned about who's moving in, rather than who's moving out.

- **Shortage of Talent**

  With almost every company out there expecting to lose a portion of their employee base through retirements, competition among employers is likely to heat up, making talented, and therefore desirable, workers more difficult to recruit and retain and more expensive due to the increased need for their skills.

- **Loss of KSAs** *Knowledge, skills, abilities*

  A key side effect to impending Boomer retirements is the collective loss of knowledge, skills, and abilities (KSAs). After having been entrenched in the workforce for decades, Boomers often occupy positions that require a high level of technical expertise, business acumen or, at the very least, industry experience. As younger generations move into the positions vacated by the Boomers, the odds that these new workers will be able to function at the same level as their experienced and knowledgeable predecessors are very low, and succession planning therefore becomes a critical concern.

  Presently, there are 3.3 million job openings in the United States, but roughly half of employers say they're having a hard time finding qualified workers. The skills gap is starkest in the areas of STEM (science, technology, engineering, mathematics) careers. President Obama's Council on Jobs and Competitiveness identified this gap between higher education and workforce training as a "critical problem."

- **Loss of Experience**

  The KSA vacuum plays into another business concern: lost experience. Even if a recent college graduate can demonstrate the technical or business skills necessary for a position, how can businesses replace the savvy, historical perspective of their former employees? The answer is that they cannot. Some experience can be passed on with mentoring programs and other succession planning efforts, but most companies have made meager attempts to implement such programs. According to a 2013 survey by InterSearch Worldwide, 55 percent of executives from 34 countries say their companies don't have a process for conducting CEO succession planning. And according to the 2012 *Fortune* article, "When Leaders

Are Scarce Employees Look to Peers," only 25 percent of large U.S. companies have peer-mentoring programs.

- **Younger Management**

  If you're a Boomer (1946–1964) you might be thinking you won't have to concern yourself with any of this because you'll soon be happily retired, sipping on pina coladas by the pool. But let's face it. Our nation's economy isn't booming and retirement is expensive. As a result, economists predict more than 80 percent of Boomers will have to work past the age of 65 because they don't have enough money to retire. That means at some point you could find yourself working for a younger boss. It will be a reality similar to the plot portrayed in the 2004 movie, *In Good Company*, about a middle-aged executive (Dennis Quaid) answering to a new boss who is half his age (Topher Grace).

Like it or not, ready or not, the fact remains that workplace demographics are changing. The biggest concern to every business in every sector in every corner of the world should be whether the next generation is getting the jobs, experience, and security they need to move the economy forward. The world needs to worry a whole lot less about the Boomers leaving (because they will) and worry a whole lot more about whether they've adequately prepared Generation Y to be the best economic engine possible (because we need them to be).

Here are a few of the ways associations are helping young professionals get the jobs and skills they need to succeed:

When Jonge Noordelijke Ondernemers (Young Northern Entrepreneurs) in Holland shifted its focus on meeting the needs of its members—personally and professionally—the association observed membership growth of 200 percent in just two years. Abe Brandsma of Jong Management (Holland) said emphasis is moving from training members how to move up in a company to focusing on what moves someone on a personal level to pursue a certain ambition. As an association for business owners, Jong Management gives members an opportunity to visit companies, engage in debates, and organize conferences and trade missions.

The Bar Association of San Francisco provides recent graduates with training, pro bono work experience, mentorship, and debt reduction information as part of the association's Mind the Gap program. The bar also plans to offer training in the business skills needed by the many young lawyers who are opening their own practices because they can't find jobs.

Claudio Kuo, vice president and treasurer of the Red Cross Student Desk in The Hague, Netherlands, said 60 active student members are responsible for planning and executing local events and fundraising activities and doing daily-based volunteering. While some are very experienced in fundraising and charity work, others have no experience. The advantage to being involved is the opportunity to learn valuable skills and to truly make a difference.

Nancy Degan, chair of the American Bar Association's (ABA's) Section of Litigation, is introducing a law school outreach program. This involves member leaders in the ABA Section of Litigation presenting programs at law schools on such topics as "How to get a job in a law firm" and "How to be a superstar associate." In connection with presenting the programs, ABA leaders will present a video or other presentation on all the benefits to law students and lawyers of belonging to the Section of Litigation. "Our hope is that by having these future lawyers join while in law school, they will see the value of membership, and continue to retain their membership once they are out practicing," Degan said.

Turnover

Generation Y is typically identified as being a fickle and wavering group of individuals. Here today, gone tomorrow. Job-hopping. Young and restless. Anyway you describe it, Generation Y is known for moving out or moving on within about a two-year time period. Studies show that Gen Y employees are demanding more from employers and if their needs aren't met, they look for greener pastures. In fact, turnover among Generation Y is about twice as high in comparison to older generations.

According to the 2013 PayScale and Millennial Branding Generations at Work Study, an estimated 15 percent of managers fall into the Generation Y age category, and managers generally cost more to replace. High turnover among Gen Y managers will do nothing less than create chaos.

A Gen Y research firm, Millennial Branding, attributes the greatest amount of turnover to workplace culture. Gen Y workers seek a strong and meaningful workplace culture—and beyond Google and a handful of other exceptional employee-first, innovation-driven work cultures—many companies fall short of providing great places to work where employees are making an impact and building meaningful relationships.

Other reasons Generation Y jumps ship, according to the 2013 *Cost of Millennial Retention* study, include receiving a better offer (30 percent), feeling their career goals aren't aligned with the company (27 percent), and sensing a lack of career opportunities (13 percent).

Young workers are always questioning whether their current employers will be able to support and invest in them for the long term. If Ys don't trust their manager or company to provide stable employment, career enrichment, and progression, the relationship will be transactional at best. Trust is a necessity for Generation Y.

What drives Gen Y crazy is being overlooked because of their age or lack of experience. This generation strongly believes in evaluating people based on skills and performance, not experience or tenure.

Many established organizations—associations included—reward people for the length of time spent in a particular role. Older generations tend to think in terms of quantity because tenure represented loyalty, dedication, and wisdom—all values to the Boomer generation.

Generation Y is the opposite in every way. They always think in terms of quality because they've been raised in a rapidly changing uber-competitive marketplace. They value speed, service, skills, and a competitive advantage. They believe the best person should get the job regardless of age or years of experience. In addition, Gen Y isn't likely to stay at a company for five years, and they certainly won't wait that long for a promotion. This mobile generation wants a mobile career. In other words, they want their employers to allow them to literally move around the company into new jobs or assignments every 12 to 24 months. This need to implement a career lattice rather than a ladder is challenging employers as they try to create more talent mobility, special assignments, and job rotation programs.

A few years ago, I met with the human resources director of a large restaurant franchise. She was sharing with me all the perks the company provided to Generation Y, and she was perplexed as to why turnover was happening. Then she told me employees are required to enroll in a three-year leadership development program in order to be eligible for a promotion.

Turns out the company's leadership track was the equivalent of an MBA program including three years of extensive travel, training, overtime, executive presentations, and research. Bottom line, Generation Y won't be interested in a multi-year program trying to prove themselves worthy of promotion. It's entirely too long of a commitment! Nor will the instant-gratification, multi-tasking generation stay in a stagnant, hierarchical environment just twiddling their thumbs and waiting for an opportunity to move up. Mobility and results are essential elements to engaging Generation Y.

Not surprising, data shows a key difference between Generation Y and other generations is their desire to move rapidly and their willingness to embark on short-term assignments. Older employees prefer to take growth at a slower pace and tend to focus on long-term growth.

Knowing what engages this generation is important because the loss of young employees is very costly. The Millennial Branding survey found that 87 percent of companies reported it costs between $15,000 and $25,000 to replace each Gen Y employee.

Losing Gen Y workers results in a loss of relevance and fresh ideas, an understanding of the younger consumer demographic, and an ability to match product ideas with emerging market opportunities. It's also a loss of future business growth as companies are forced to continually address the rotation of leadership. Organizations need a management development pipeline; without that pipeline, companies will have a difficult time growing long term.

To stop job migration from Gen Y, associations can help member companies really focus on improving their workplace cultures and investing in the careers of their young employees. By providing services or training on workplace flexibility options, mentoring programs, employee recognition, community service programs, and intrapreneurship (allowing employees to become entrepreneurs and develop new products and services for the company), associations can help companies engage their Y employees.

Holly Portner, executive director at Minnesota Collegiate DECA (formerly the Distributive Education Clubs of America) emphasized that Generation Y's knack for entrepreneurism must be taken into consideration by employers and nurtured. "They have a strong desire to own something," Portner said.

Some of DECA's programs, which are business-focused, have expanded significantly with Generation Y's arrival because of their strong interest to learn about business, including how to fund and market a business. She adds that any opportunity to develop skilled Gen Y workers will become a "huge resource" for corporations.

Leadership Development

Generation Y wants to lead. Actually, they are less interested in running your company than running their own, which is why they've been referred to as the most entrepreneurial generation.

As this book has already addressed, it's pretty clear why this has happened. To recap, this generation grew up in an economy where their parents and older peers went through a massive recession and may have been laid off. They've seen rapid growth in start-up companies and the struggles larger organizations have faced. In fact, they've seen the fall of entire companies, like Enron, due to unethical practices.

So Ys are driven to lead, and they tend to believe they would make better leaders than other generations. However, Generation Y also recognizes they aren't really ready to lead. In a series of global studies on this generation, Deloitte's 2013 Millennial Survey identified they wanted and needed leadership assignments as well as training and coaching. There are two opportunities for associations here. One is to give young professionals the leadership training and coaching they need. Another is to help member companies understand and meet the expectations of these emerging leaders.

Leadership means something different to Generation Y. They are comfortable with transparency and they believe leadership should be the same. They want to work for leaders that offer openness, inclusion, and diversity and that's how they will lead, as well. One of the ways this generation does this, of course, is through social media. This is why internal blogs and wikis and various corporate social networks are so widely used by them, and often not by Boomers.

I recently worked with a well-known household goods company on a strategy for engaging Generation Y. When I shared with the company's leadership that former employees—including managers—had been using glassdoor.com to post negative reviews about their employment experiences, the leaders were shocked and embarrassed. They weren't familiar with the site and couldn't believe how unhappy these former Gen Y employees were or how public they went with their opinions.

If you want to attract and retain young professionals, the top leaders must be open and transparent and also realize that the organization doesn't control the message anymore—Generation Y does.

As was mentioned under the section on turnover, Generation Y wants to try new roles and projects every 12 to 24 months. This means for the first time ever, organizations have to create a dynamic, assignment-based career model to develop young high-potential professionals.

Don't underestimate the significance of this shift. For the first time in history, leadership isn't related to experience or the length of time spent working in a job or at a company. Leadership potential is now based on skills, drive, vision, innovation, and the ability to naturally get others to follow you. Therefore, organizations need to think less about time spent on the job and more about creating a series of assignments, each of which help young leaders improve their skills.

As an ASAE University facilitator for the Certificate in Association Management, Maria Huntley interacts with many young professionals and associations. She believes associations are woefully behind in giving young professionals leadership experience and influence. "Don't have one 'young professional' on the board as a token member," she said. She encourages associations to develop a board that's half composed of experienced members and half composed of young professionals and students, bringing a balance of experience and innovation to the boardroom.

Gen Y at Work

Think about the rapidity of change in the global economy, global politics, and consumer technology in the past five years. If change continues at its current rate, let alone accelerates, it's going to completely redefine the concept of work and leadership. For the industries and companies that have struggled to make change and adapt, this means inevitable failure. We can't get stuck in the past. Change is the only certainty.

It's obvious that Generation Y's arrival, accompanied by some of the biggest economic shifts, will certainly usher in widespread and significant change in the workplace. Here are a few changes associations need to anticipate now and take the lead in helping their member companies prepare:

- **Collaboration**
  As noted above, leadership is going to get a lot more complex. It's going to be less about authority and more about influence. Collaboration will rule because younger generations have been groomed to do it, cycle times will demand it, and technology will continue to enable it.

- **Technology**
  The workforce of the future will be innovation-centered, highly productive, and a magnet for global talent. New technologies will be developed and globalization will continue to drive the utilization of advanced mobile technologies. Expect increased telecommuting, virtual teams, and more work flexibility overall. (Plus, the arrival of 3D printing and presentations, robots, space travel, and holograms— but perhaps your association is still warming up to the idea of getting an app.)

- **Skills**
  Knowledge won't be the competitive advantage anymore. With technology, knowledge is quickly outdated and accessible to all in real-time. The critical skills needed to be successful in the new working environment are vision and foresight to anticipate or respond

to change very quickly, make wise decisions, and take action to create a better future.

• Customization by Generation

With three distinct generations in the workforce—Baby Boomers, Generation X, and Generation Y—employers will need to develop highly individualized solutions to accommodate the career needs of each generation. Savvy business owners and chief executives will take advantage of the skills, attitudes, and unique characteristics of each group and create career paths for all three generations so they see how they have a future with your firm.

• Diversity

In addition to the generational shift, our nation will witness gender and racial shifts, as well. According to Pew Research Center, women are moving into the role of breadwinner and also more likely to get a college education. Presently, some 4 in 10 American households with children under the age of 18 include a mother who is either the sole or primary earner for her family. The percentage of women attending college has been on the rise since 1994 and now outnumbers the percentage of men attending college. According to Pew Research Center, 71 percent of women enrolled in college in 2012 immediately following high school compared to 61 percent for men. Hispanic and black women are outpacing the number of Hispanic and black men in college by 13 percent and 12 percent, respectively. Racial and ethnic shifts in the population are more concentrated in younger generations because most immigrants are young adults and because Hispanic families living in the United States tend to have more than the average number of children.

• Mobilization

Generation Y is highly entrepreneurial, so we're likely to see more start-ups and small businesses, which will spur corporate downsizing. We will not see long careers of 10 or more years in one company anymore, but maybe 6 years with employees making either functional or geographic changes every 2 years.

• Loyalty

Loyalty is to people and not companies, and time is more valued than money. This means Generation Y will want flexible schedules and may prefer additional vacation days to cash bonuses.

Fast-paced change in our society has affected all industries and will continue to change the nature of work for the next 10 to 15 years. Chances are if your organization isn't thinking about the future, it's already irrelevant. Everything about how we work and do business will change if it hasn't already. The chart identifies some of the core areas where the workforce and the perception of work are changing alongside the arrival of Gen Y.

WORK BEFORE Y	WORK SINCE Y
Experience and tenure	Skills and performance
Controlled	Transparent
Long-term	Short-term
Career ladder	Career lattice
Jobs	Projects
Stability	Change
Tradition	Innovation

All of this change is happening for a reason. Older generations look at the behaviors of younger generations and complain they have no loyalty or long-term job commitment. But this book has cited numerous examples of how shifting economies drive shifts in values, and this is no exception. Generation Y does approach work and define work from a very different place than previous generations for these reasons:

- **No job security**
  An unstable economy has caused Gen Y to devalue the tenure of a position. Even if you stayed with the same company for 30 years, what's the payoff for remaining when benefits, pensions, and investments are not guaranteed?

- **Changing loyalty**
  A company gets what it gives. Amidst mergers, downsizing, and negativity or resistance to hiring Ys, companies have become less loyal to their employees. Generation Y hasn't known employers to behave any differently, so as employees they are less loyal to the companies.

- **More choices**
  Generation Y is a very adventurous generation. They crave exploring the next opportunity to discover, create, and expand. Sometimes

called dreamers; this generation has an entrepreneurial nature that searches for freedom, limitlessness, and fulfillment. Sometimes referred to as entitled, this generation was provided for and raised receiving more and therefore expecting more. This sense of privilege is the result of having more choices and protection in their young lives. As a result, they lack patience and are more willing to seek out and move on to another opportunity.

Functioning in a workplace dominated by Gen Y will be a very different experience for Boomers and Gen Xers (1965–1981) who both tend to be success-driven, strong individualists, and independent thinkers. In contrast, Ys are driven to make a difference, function well in teams, and are highly social creatures.

As more Ys move into management, we can expect some major changes to occur, such as more women promoted to leadership, redesigned offices to allow for open-concept work spaces, telecommuting as the norm, and social platforms used to manage daily employee performance.

Sonja Moseley, 27, is the Director of Certification & Benefits for the Marine Retailers Association of the Americas (MRAA) and former executive director of Arizona Parks and Recreation Association. She wrote an article for the XYZ University blog on the value that Generation Y employees bring to an association. The following is an excerpt from her article:

> After 20+ years of Baby Boomer generation leadership, a 30-something Matt Gruhn (president) took the reins at MRAA in 2011. Since then, membership has grown over 200 percent! Prior to his leadership at MRAA, Matt played a crucial role in reviving the Marine Dealer Conference and Expo. Under his direction, participation grew from 97 (attendees) in 2007 to more than 1,100 in 2013 and we expect continued growth this year.
>
> In addition to Matt's palpable enthusiasm, he has surrounded himself with young professionals and fresh ideas. Our staff is all 40 years old or younger, with two thirds of us in our 20s.
>
> Michael Geatz, our marketing coordinator, is fresh out of college and overflowing with new ideas. In the world of marketing, tools and technology are changing at an increasingly rapid pace. His ability to navigate through multiple realms of member engagement and recruitment has most certainly contributed to our massive membership growth and conference participation.
>
> Another interesting avenue for younger engagement at MRAA is the role of the Young Leaders Advisory Council (YLAC). YLAC was created in 2009 to engage the next generation of marine dealers. Since then, YLAC has played a critical role in moving the association forward. In addition, this

group has funneled young professionals to board positions, allowing for a stronger voice from future industry leaders.

I have no doubt that a large part of our momentum here at MRAA is correlated to the young, refreshing and unconstrained atmosphere.

At MRAA, not only are young professionals encouraged to play important roles, they are given the freedom to carry out these roles in their own way. If you are looking for big results, do not be afraid to hire young professionals and set them loose. You may be surprised by the results.

Does your association know the average age of its membership? If you don't, I would encourage you to figure it out through membership surveys. I've worked with many associations with average membership ages ranging between 48 and 58 years old. One association that really stuck with me had an *industry* average age of 60 years old. This association stuck with me because I knew they wouldn't survive much longer as an association or an industry.

The fact is, for an industry with an average age of 60, the chances of reversing the aging trend at this point borders on the impossible; they are too far gone.

What I can't help wondering is, what has this industry been doing for the past 10 years? How did it get to this point? Didn't they ever stop to ponder the concept of change or to consider that they desperately needed to build a bench of young talent? Don't make this same mistake.

One thing is certain. All over the world, the NEETs and freeters and boomerang kids are hungry for a chance to thrive. And soon, companies everywhere are going to need this generation to survive. When that time comes and the tables have turned, will your association and the employers your association represents be the ones this generation chooses?

Here's a hint: If your association or the industry it represents continues to neglect this generation, don't count on them to show up for work tomorrow. They will probably be out causing a revolution, starting up their own company, or working for someone who cared about their futures when it seemed they didn't have one.

According to the U.S. Bureau of Labor Statistics, the following industries are aging the fastest, based on median industry employee age.

Real Estate

Median industry age: 49

Only 6 percent of real estate agents are under the age of 34.

Insurance

Median industry age: 45

While 84 percent of insurance industry employers have job openings, they are struggling to find experienced workers and battling a negative reputation among Gen Ys as an irrelevant, aging, and boring industry.

Manufacturing

Median industry age: 45

With an estimated 600,000 empty jobs, the industry is struggling to find skilled workers and Gen Ys who are interested in doing what's perceived to be laborious, tedious, dangerous, dirty work.

Healthcare

Median industry age: 43

By 2020, half of all registered nurses will be retirement age.

Top Fortune 500 Industries for the Number of Workers over 50:

- Airlines
- Utilities
- Insurance
- Retail
- Chemicals
- Aerospace and defense
- Packaging and containers
- Forest and paper products
- Food production
- Beverages

CHAPTER 9

Benefits or Bust

*"I'm not a member of any association at this time.
I guess I haven't come into contact with an association
that struck me as one that I would really benefit
from through membership. The fact is, for me and
my generation, we expect the association to give us
something in order for us to give our time in return."*

Megan Shankle
Association Industry Specialist, ISG Solutions
Age: 32

Selling shoes was a sensible business, but the CEO of this shoe company didn't want it to be about the shoes. Anybody could sell shoes. This had to be bigger, better, meaningful, and inspirational. This had to blow the competition out of the water.

Yes, I'm talking about shoes. But Zappos didn't become a billion dollar company by selling shoes alone; Tony Hsieh instead focused his entire business on creating a "wow" customer service experience. This dedication to service became a mission, and everyone from Zappos' suppliers to employees to customers became missionaries for the brand.

Early on, Hsieh took the unconventional path in more ways than one. Here are just a few of the ways he grew a business renowned for service:

- Free shipping is offered both ways along with a 365-day return policy. Customers can order 10 pairs of shoes, try them on, and send them all back. Free.

- Call times are not measured. A call center chat that continues for an hour with no sale is no crime. The payoff? The representative has the customer's undivided attention for that hour and the customer is likely to return next time with a sale. (For Zappos, that's the equivalent of 5,000 leisurely calls a day!)

- Every item dropped into a customer's online shopping cart is guaranteed to be in stock and available.

- Shipping is promised in five to six days. But Zappos automatically upgrades almost every order to free overnight shipping.

- The warehouse operates 24/7. Perhaps that's economically unsound, but it's ultimately beneficial to the customer experience. Some items arrive on a customer's doorstep in as little as eight hours.

- The company spends little on marketing and advertising, opting to invest in the customer experience, which fosters repeat business and word of mouth advertising.

- To ensure new hires really want to be a part of the Zappos culture, Hsieh offers every new hire $2,000 to quit. Hardly anyone takes the money.

After debuting as the highest-ranking newcomer in *Fortune*'s annual Best Companies to Work For list in 2009, Zappos was acquired by Amazon in a deal valued at over $1.2 billion on the day of closing.

Zappos remains best known for its commitment to provide the best customer service possible. An excellent example of the Sharing, Experience, and Impact economies, Zappos proved that by concentrating on the happiness of customers and others around you, you can dramatically increase your success.

Happiness. Rewards. Service. These are the common themes throughout the book. Just as Zappos wasn't about selling shoes, your association isn't about selling memberships. This has to be bigger, better, meaningful, and inspirational. This had to blow the competition out of the water. Let's start with why.

Why Does Your Association Exist?

Does your association exist to protect the industry, advocate, or build a community of stakeholders?

If any of these answers sound like a good fit, then you are probably headed down the wrong path.

- First of all, protecting the industry, advocating, and building a community of stakeholders doesn't address any of Generation Y's needs. Protecting the industry doesn't inspire, tap into personal happiness, and may or may not make a difference for others.

- Second, none of the statements I offered up will succeed at differentiating your association from all the competitors out there.

- Third, members join your association because they believe your association can help them solve a problem. Actually, this ties back to personal happiness. If you can do something to substantially improve the lives of your members, minimize their frustrations, and deliver a really positive experience, your organization will always come out on top.

Associations have this tendency to speak and act like mission statements all the time. It's this broad, sweeping, eyes-glazing-over, vague approach that always seems to fall short of expectations and never really packs a punch.

Here's an example of one association's Statement of Purpose, found on the association's Join page of the website. This is a large and influential association. The statement is entirely too long weighing in at six paragraphs. If someone is interested in joining—especially a Gen Y—chances are they aren't going to read through a lengthy description. The first paragraph matters most. As you read the following paragraph ask yourself—how would joining this association make a difference in my life or the lives of others? (I've omitted some of the wording to protect this association's identity.)

> The Association is the only full-service professional organization representing the nation's entire ... population. From the halls of Congress and federal agencies to the boardrooms, (and other) facilities, The Association is the strongest voice for the profession. It is headquartered in City, State.

There is nothing here to indicate this association's membership is better or different, important and necessary. Moreover, it doesn't speak to *me*, how the association is focused on solving my challenges, or making my life better.

Generation Y, also known as the YOLO and Trophy Kids generation, will always want to know how your association will impact their lives personally. They could care less about the "nation's entire population" or the "strongest voice" as in the example above. Remember, it's about quality not quantity. It's about me (the member), not you (the association).

According to Simon Sinek, author of *Start With Why* (2009), organizations need to inspire people in order to effectively compete, grow, and succeed, and the best way to do that is to start with why. Zappos succeeded because the company existed to deliver exceptional customer service and happiness. Not shoes. Service is Zappos' why. Likewise

Starbucks doesn't focus on selling coffee. As we discussed earlier in this book, Starbucks exists "to inspire and nurture the human spirit—one person, one cup, and one neighborhood at a time."

If your association wants to succeed, it must start with why and Y—one relies on the other. For the love of Gen Y, make it meaningful, motivational, and memorable. Make it your association's focus to make a difference. Here are some examples of association mission statements that have started with why.

American Public Works Association

The American Public Works Association (APWA) exists to develop and support the people, agencies, and organizations that plan, build, maintain, and improve our communities. Working together, APWA and its membership contribute to a higher and sustainable quality of life.

Energy Users Association of Australia

The Energy Users Association of Australia was formed in 1996 to provide a single national association to effectively represent and service the needs of Australian energy users. We exist to assist our members run efficient and profitable businesses as they relate to their energy use.

National Furniture Movers and Storage Association (NFMSA)

Customers want to trust their mover. Many unprofessional operators only exist by under-cutting legal business. The NFMSA offers your business the opportunity to demonstrate that your company can be trusted. The benefit to the consumer is a greater chance the move will go smoothly and the benefit to the member is greater sales.

Professional Photographers of America

More photographers get into the industry everyday, but few know how to profitably run a business and many don't know where to turn for support. That's why Professional Photographers of America was started back in 1869, and that's why we exist today.

It is the cause—the why—that inspires loyalty. Instead of asking *what* your association must do to compete in this rapidly changing world, start by asking these two questions:

- *Why* did our association organize in the first place?

- *What* can we do to keep our *why* relevant considering all the changes and opportunities that have emerged with the arrival of Generation Y?

Great associations will be able to keep the why relevant to a younger audience. Great associations will be capable of leading people, changing the course of industries, and benefitting lives in the process. The only way to achieve this is to focus on members first.

Members First

With the most protected, YOLO, and Trophy generation moving into power, there's a definite focus on, well, "Me." They are products of their environments in more ways than one. As children of the Boomers, once dubbed the Me Generation, they've always had access to multi-media and customization. This generation expects great service and tremendous ROI (return on investment). Not surprising, Generation Y wants to know "What's in it for *me?*"

Like it or not, that Me-Centric approach is here to stay. On the upside, Generation Y usually follows up the question, "How will this make a difference in my life?" with the question "How will my participation make a difference in the lives of others?" But their decision to join hinges on your answer to the first question, and that requires associations to move from taking a passive approach to membership (people will join because it's the right thing to do), to taking an intentional approach accompanied by delivering great ROI and a great membership experience.

To Generation Y, ROI comes in the form of happiness, rewards, and service.

- **Happiness**

  Zappos put a premium on happiness from the very beginning. The result is a customer base that doesn't just buy shoes because they need them, but shops at Zappos because the entire experience is a positive one. Order a pair of sneakers and the box arrives in days. It's bright yellow and covered in the word "happy."

  Generation Y will not respond well to tactics or messages rooted in negativity or criticism and they won't embrace anything ambiguous or meaningless. They always want to know how a membership in your association will make their lives better; how their purchase will reward them by providing something of value to themselves or to others. This trophy mentality will often come into play in Gen Y's buying decisions.

The Young Aviation Professionals (YAP) group at the Air Traffic Controllers Association (ATCA) hosts YAPPY Hours. The YAPs are encouraged to bring their friends in aviation and the event features food in a casual atmosphere. Once a very hierarchical association, ATCA has started recruiting young professionals for committees and is finding ways to give them opportunities to meet and mingle with executives. While the YAP group is new, Peter Dumont, president and CEO of ATCA, said the association's main goal is to "find out what members want and create it" while bridging the gaps and building community between young professionals and experienced aviation professionals.

- **Rewards**
  Many retailers, businesses, and now apps are using rewards programs—the version of a trophy for Gen Y. A consumer example is the Starbucks Rewards program. Customers in the My Starbucks Reward program can earn "Stars" by paying with their registered cards, engaging with the brand's mobile app, buying coffee in grocery stores, and even engaging with the brand through their various social channels and public promotions. Once Stars are earned, they are stored in a customer's user profile until they are redeemed for drinks, food items, and more.

- **Service**
  Gen Y wants personalized, knowledgeable human interaction when they come to your association's website, event, or office. They want to see that the association is connected to their needs and has a commitment to customer service with adequate staff present to address issues and solve problems. They also want that personal touch—a thank you for their business and a request that they come again.

The Value Zone

In addition to happiness, rewards, and service, Generation Y's decision to join is tied to their values. This book has addressed the emergence of several economic shifts, and those economic shifts prove that all of your members' values, regardless of age, are shifting. Here's an overview of each of the economies and how these economies are shifting values and expectations.

	IN	OUT
SHARING	Access and collaboration	Ownership and acquisition
GIG	Multi-careerism and entrepreneurs	One-career employees and loyalty
KNOWLEDGE	Innovation, interconnectedness, globalization	Automation, silos, regimentation
EXPERIENCE	Emotion and experiences as commodities	Products and services as commodities
IMPACT	For-benefit enterprises, grassroots	For-profit enterprises, advocacy

It's really important to understand that Generation Y has come of age during these economies and isn't familiar with or especially fond of anything listed in the out row. That means if your association wants to be relevant to this generation, you must focus entirely on the in row. That's where meaning and relevance reside to this generation and nowhere else.

Member value is defined as the perceived trade-off between benefits (what members receive) versus sacrifices (what members give). While member value is shifting for all generations, the Trickle-Up Effect means that shift is most evident within Generation Y. So we look to Y as an indicator of future change.

First, sacrifices. Let's face it. Generation Y's threshold for sacrifices is quite low, especially in the learning or early stages of membership. This is the instant-gratification, internet, and credit card-raised generation that wants everything to be accessible, convenient, and fast. They're busy and broke to boot, so sacrifices have to be at a minimum. Your association must find ways to be more affordable, convenient, and responsive or it will never get to the stage of must-have membership with Generation Y.

Next, benefits. Here, too, Generation Y has high expectations. These are the trophy kids, after all. They have always been recognized for participation and not achievement. This means that simply by participating in your association—whether it's just showing up for an event, joining, or volunteering—this generation demands something in return. They demand it because they're used to it.

Now we can move into the value zone. Members will experience the highest value when all three of the following are represented:

- **Personal values and goals**

  This means the association's membership meets the member's personal values and goals. I've already mentioned that great benefits for Generation Y are focused on happiness, rewards, and service. To take that a step further, consider that people are more likely to join an association when they believe that association can help them solve a problem. For Generation Y, most of their problems currently revolve around careers and finances, so products, services, and benefits focused on helping them secure employment, learn skills, and gain leadership experience will be personally valuable to them. I can't emphasize enough how important it is for associations to investigate for themselves what their Gen Y members need. That dialogue is key to building knowledge about Generation Y and relationships with the demographic you are trying to reach.

  One association I worked with couldn't understand why the Generation Y members were dropping off the grid. Membership was declining for the first time in years and the association couldn't understand why until they surveyed and interviewed Gen Y members. They were surprised to learn a growing number of young members wanted help launching start-up businesses. The association didn't offer this type of service and, unbeknownst to them, was quickly becoming irrelevant among the Y membership.

- **Use Situation**

  Every member carefully considers how the membership will be used and whether there is enough use and benefit to be gained by purchasing the membership. As you now know, Generation Y makes decisions on where to live and work based on convenience and community-building opportunities. They want to access information quickly via your association's website and they will also take both time and money into careful consideration. For example, a Gen Y might not be willing—or able—to take a few hours off during the day to attend an association lunch, and may not be able to afford the $50 for the association lunches. Both situations will affect the use, and therefore the value, of the membership for Gen Y.

- **Perception**

  If the association is perceived to be outdated, irrelevant, unfriendly, or aging, Generation Y isn't likely to join. Perception is partially based on brand and partially based on service. In the last chapter I mentioned that both manufacturing and insurance as industries are struggling to engage young talent simply because both industries are suffering from a perception that isn't favorable to Gen Y.

This generation would rather live at home than risk working in a miserable job. They outright refuse to engage in organizations that deliver negative experiences or even those organizations that are believed to deliver negative experiences.

If the member doesn't have a positive interaction with the person she speaks to on the phone or feels like she doesn't belong when attending an event, the degree of trust and belonging she feels will take a turn for the worse. At that point, it's nearly impossible to win Gen Y's favor. This generation is big on first impressions and not a fan of second chances.

The diagram shows how value is evident when personal goals, use, and perceptions are met.

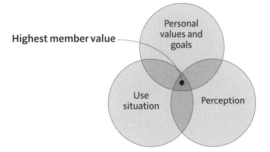

The key difference between good associations and great associations is their willingness to go above and beyond the normal order of doing business to answer their members' needs.

When you can identify *why* members should join, put your members first and make a difference in their lives, your association will be considered valuable and membership will undoubtedly grow.

Bottom line: Your association has already made history. If your association wants to live on, there is no past. There's only future. You must adapt to the changing marketplace and build your association with the future in mind. And it has to be bigger, better, meaningful, and inspirational. It has to blow the competition out of the water. Then, and only then, will you engage the membership of Generation Y.

CHAPTER 10

Make It Count

*"My generation believes we can change the
world. But the fact is, we can get somewhere
far better by working together."*

**Emily Woody Bibens, CAE
Woody Bibens and Associates
Age: 29**

Detroit has gone through a major economic and demographic decline
in recent decades. CNN reports the city has lost over 60 percent of its
population since 1950. The automobile industry has suffered from global
competition and has moved much of its remaining production out of the
city. As a result, huge areas of the city are in a state of severe urban decay.

In 2013, Detroit filed the largest municipal bankruptcy case in U.S.
history. Not surprising, the city has one of the highest unemployment
rates in the nation and has lost most of its young talent. The organization,
Challenge Detroit, has evolved with a simple mission: to attract and
retain really great talent back to Detroit. But it has dared to go where no
other city has gone before, taking a whole new approach to stimulating
Detroit's economy. It's a program that is staking its success on a generation
of people with ideas, motivation, creativity, and a whole lot of guts. This
program isn't a sure success; it's a risk and a significant challenge. And
it's not for the faint of heart. It's for people who want to make a genuinely
impactful change in a city that's in desperate need of it.

Each year, Challenge Detroit calls for people to step up and dedicate
one year to live, work, play, and give, all while documenting their
experiences in Detroit. The applicants, mostly Gen Ys and all college
educated, compete for grants that will allow them to participate in the
challenge.

The program selects 30 fellows from a pool of hundreds of applicants.

Fellows are matched with host companies—like General Motors,
Detroit Lions, and CBS Detroit Radio—where they'll work four days a
week and make $36,000 for the year plus benefits. They are required to

work on 10 community projects throughout the year, which could range from working on the development of after-school programs to developing an environmental sustainability strategy for the city.

Fellows also receive access to Detroit cultural and entertainment events, take part in a leadership training program, participate in 10 team challenges over the course of a year, receive a $500 per month stipend for living expenses, and live near one another to build a community among them. Twenty-four of the 27 fellows who took part in Challenge Detroit's first Fellows class stayed in Detroit—five who started their own companies.

I love what executive director Deirdre Greene Groves has to say about the program as something that makes a difference in more ways than one and makes Detroit "better than the way we found it." As she put it: "Detroit can withstand the hurt as much as it can offer up opportunity." And so can your association. If an entire city can mobilize its business and community sectors and achieve change, your association can, too.

Research indicates a third of New Year's resolutions never make it to the end of January. I think that's because most of us approach resolutions as wishes and desires and not as goals. This is true in our personal lives as well as our nation's institutions. Even amidst economic upheaval, rapidly changing technology, and unprecedented demographic shifts, many organizations are clinging to traditions and processes of the past. The leaders of these organizations may say they want change, but they don't actually stick to a strategy to make change happen. This isn't surprising. Actually, the lack of change is evident in all sectors. Here are just a few examples reported by the sources in the past few years:

- 70 percent is average expected loss of members to retirement by 2021 (Association Adviser)

- 64 percent of directors at S&P 500 firms are 60 or older; 15 percent older than 69 (Bloomberg News)

- 62 percent of nonprofit board members are over the age of 50 (BoardSource)

- 60 is the average age of a U.S. Senator—the oldest in history (NBC News)

- 55 is the average age in the U.S. House of Representatives—oldest in 100 years (NBC News)

- 55 is the median age for a S&P 500 CEO (CEO Statistics)

• 23 percent of Canadian associations have a next-generation strategy (Greenfield Services)

The fact is, change isn't easy. It also isn't optional.

Generation Y's move into power is already spurring shifts, which you have read about in this book. But we're not anywhere near the end. In fact, we're likely to see a great global redistribution of economic and social power in the near future, as power moves away from traditional institutions that have failed to deliver progress and towards the organization whose leaders understand and act on the big trends shaping our future. In other words, the phrase "Change or Die" is more accurate than ever before.

Jim Nagel, an experienced association executive, urges his peers to take Generation Y's involvement very seriously. "What will your legacy become if you worked at an association for 50 years and made zero impact? You can't accept the status quo. It's broken and needs to be fixed. You've got to teach someone else to fish."

If survival isn't enough to inspire your organization to change, then perhaps these three strategies will help your leadership set goals, embrace change, and achieve success. I added in recommended timelines to help your association incrementally and successfully achieve change.

Know Y: 30 Days

The whole purpose of this book is to help you learn more about Generation Y, but you really need to know Y for yourself to know why they aren't engaging in your association. In the 1990s, the New York Police Commissioner made his top brass—including himself—ride the subways day and night, to understand why frightened New Yorkers had come to call it the "Electric Sewer." Today, we see similar concepts play out on CBS' *Undercover Boss* reality show. The point is, you can advocate for change until you're blue in the face, but lecturing doesn't always work.

In the next 30 days:

Look for ways to get the decision makers to experience the harsh realities that make change necessary. Start by bringing the board or senior executives face-to-face with students and young professionals in Generation Y. Also, during the next 30 days, challenge your board and your stakeholders to hold 30 conversations with 30 people who are Generation Y—ages 19 to 32 in 2014.

The audience for your association is changing. The workforce is shifting, so the audience is also changing for your members and member companies. The better you understand the next generation, the more likely your association will be able to engage them and help your member companies engage them as well. Don't assume—even after reading this book—that you have all the answers. You must find out for yourself and really familiarize yourself with this audience. You must see your association through their eyes.

During the next 30 days, hold 30 conversations with 30 people who are younger than you. Don't know 30 Gen Ys? Then each time you meet with someone, ask for a referral to someone else whom that person really admires within that age range.

Be sure to ask each person the following questions:

- What organizations do you admire and why?
- What are your greatest professional challenges?
- If you could create an ideal association experience what would it be like?

Document your conversations on a spreadsheet and at the end of 30 days, meet with your fellow stakeholders to share your findings and ascertain the best path for going forward.

Know Why: 60 Days

If your association wants to succeed, you must know Y and why—one relies on the other. Now that you've taken the time to really get to know Y, you know that membership has to be meaningful, motivational, and memorable to them. So make it your association's focus to make a difference.

In the next 60 Days:

Explore these two questions with your stakeholders:

- *Why* does our association exist?
- *What* can we do to keep our *why* relevant considering all the changes and opportunities that have emerged with the arrival of Generation Y?

Review all your marketing, messaging, and other touchpoints with your audience—do they all start with why? In my last book, *The End of Membership as We Know It* (2011), I described this as the difference between talking about features (what your association does) and talking about outcomes (how membership makes a difference in members' lives).

Either way you want to look at it, your association must stop approaching everything from a membership sales position. Instead, identify ways to inspire your members by:

- Focusing on the personal happiness of members;
- Giving your members an opportunity to make a difference for others;
- Differentiating your association from all the competitors out there; and
- Solving the challenges your members currently face.

Influence Change: 90 Days

After you get clarity and know both Y and why, your association can begin to influence change. This is where the rubber hits the road and some tough decisions must be made, but your association will be more successful because of it.

In the next 90 days:

Assess the following cornerstones of your association, identify where change is needed, and make the changes needed.

- **Move into the Value Zone**

  Members will experience the highest value when all three of the following are positively represented: personal values and goals, use, and perception. It starts with meeting the values of Generation Y, and the Trickle-Up Effect moves it up to increase value for all generations of members. Here's how to identify the value triggers for your association.

  - **Personal Values and Goals**

    Identify what Gen Y members need to succeed and create products, services, member benefits, and messaging focused on these needs.

  - **Use Situation**

    Identify what Gen Y members need to engage in your association—such as online access, convenience, speed, affordability, and community building—and determine the areas where your association needs to adapt to meet these needs.

  - **Perception**

    Perception is partially based on brand and partially based on customer service. First, identify your association's brand by asking Generation Y (members and nonmembers) to describe your association in one word. What words are most often used? Are they positive or negative? Is this the brand your association wants to convey or is it something else entirely? Look for common themes and identify areas of focus. For example, if your association's brand is "old," brainstorm ways your association could change that image.

Next, identify areas in your association where service could be vastly improved. If your association's reputation and ability to engage members hinges entirely on first impressions, are all the places where those impressions occur—online and in-person— truly exceptional? Identify ways to make every interaction and experience member-centric and service-oriented.

- **Resources**

Look at where your organization spends its resources and you will find its heart. Now that you know Y and you know why, is your organization investing in the right things? The right things are those that meet the needs and expectations of Generation Y, requiring the least amount of effort for the most gain. Those sacred cows that have been fenced in "just because" need to be sent off to slaughter. You are in a fight for survival here, folks. Time is running out. Your organization must be focused, nimble, and capable for nothing less than greatness. Anything that drains resources and yields minimal results should be put on the chopping block.

- **Influencers**

I wish I had a dollar for every time someone told me the board was "moving in a different direction," or "didn't support the need for change," or "undermining the association's potential." The fact is, leadership isn't the same as being a leader. Leadership is a title, but good leaders wield influence and have the ability to get people to follow them regardless of title or role.

When you're trying to implement change, you must start with the leaders. Find the leaders in your association who have influence and vision; the ones who will help you win the hearts and minds of your Gen Y members and take the initiative needed to move your association forward.

Think of Challenge Detroit. They don't want just anyone to come in and rebuild their city; they are bringing in the most passionate and motivated people willing to dedicate a year of their lives to the cause. Start with the leaders and the influencers. Once they start supporting your association's change model, shine a spotlight on their accomplishments so others get the message. Sooner or later your association will be attracting the best of the best and the naysayers and detractors will take their negativity somewhere else.

I think the ancient philosopher, Lao Tzu said it best: "If you do not change direction, you may end up where you are heading." Do you simply wish for change to happen, or is your association being intentional about making it happen? I hope for the sake of your association, it's the latter. Because if you know anything about Generation Y, you know change is needed—and time is running out.